STUDIES IN ECONOMIC AND SOCIAL HISTORY

This series, specially commissioned by the Economic History Society, provides a guide to the current interpretations of the key themes of economic and social history in which advances have recently been made or in which there has been significant debate.

Originally entitled 'Studies in Economic History', in 1974 the series had its scope extended to include topics in social history, and the new series title, 'Studies in Economic and Social History', signalises this development.

The series gives readers access to the best work done, helps them to draw their own conclusions in major fields of study, and by means of the critical bibliography in each book guides them in the selection of further reading. The aim is to provide a springboard to further work rather than a set of pre-packaged conclusions or short-cuts.

ECONOMIC HISTORY SOCIETY

The Economic History Society, which numbers over 3000 members, publishes the *Economic History Review* four times a year (free to members) and holds an annual conference. Enquiries about membership should be addressed to the Assistant Secretary, Economic History Society, Peterhouse, Cambridge. Full-time students may join the Society at special rates.

STUDIES IN ECONOMIC AND SOCIAL HISTORY

Edited for the Economic History Society by T. C. Smout

PUBLISHED

B. W. E. Alford Depression and Recovery? British Economic Growth, 1918–1939
Michael Anderson Approaches to the History of the Western Family, 1500–1914
S. D. Chapman The Cotton Industry in the Industrial Revolution
J. A. Chartres Internal Trade in England, 1500–1700
R. A. Church The Great Victorian Boom, 1850–1873
D. C. Coleman Industry in Tudor and Stuart England
P. L. Cottrell British Overseas Investment in the Nineteenth Century
Ralph Davis English Overseas Trade, 1500–1700
M. E. Falkus The Industrialisation of Russia, 1700–1914
Peter Fearon The Origins and Nature of the Great Slump, 1929–1932
M. W. Flinn British Population Growth, 1700–1850
T. R. Gourvish Railways and the British Economy 1830–1914
John Hatcher Plague, Population and the English Economy, 1348–1530
J. R. Hay The Origins of the Liberal Welfare Reforms, 1906–1914
R. H. Hilton The Decline of Serfdom in Medieval England
E. L. Jones The Development of English Agriculture, 1815–1873
John Lovell British Trade Unions, 1875–1933
J. D. Marshall The Old Poor Law, 1795–1834
Alan S. Milward The Economic Effects of the Two World Wars on Britain
G. E. Mingay Enclosure and the Small Farmer in the Age of the Industrial Revolution
Rosalind Mitchison British Population Change Since 1860
R. J. Morris Class and Class Consciousness in the Industrial Revolution 1780–1850
A. E. Musson British Trade Unions, 1800–1875
R. B. Outhwaite Inflation in Tudor and Early Stuart England
P. L. Payne British Entrepreneurship in the Nineteenth Century
Michael E. Rose The Relief of Poverty, 1834–1914
S. B. Saul The Myth of the Great Depression, 1873–1896
Arthur J. Taylor Laissez-faire and State Intervention in Nineteenth-century Britain
Peter Temin Causal Factors in American Economic Growth in the Nineteenth Century
Margaret Walsh The American Frontier Revisited

OTHER TITLES ARE IN PREPARATION

Railways
and the British Economy
1830—1914

Prepared for
The Economic History Society by

T. R. GOURVISH
Senior Lecturer in Economic and Social History
University of East Anglia

M

© The Economic History Society 1980

All rights reserved. No part of this publication may be reproduced or transmitted, in any form or by any means, without permission.

First published 1980 by
THE MACMILLAN PRESS LTD
London and Basingstoke
Associated companies in Delhi Dublin
Hong Kong Johannesburg Lagos Melbourne
New York Singapore and Tokyo

Printed in Great Britain by
J. W. Arrowsmith Ltd., Bristol BS3 2NT

British Library Cataloguing in Publication Data

Gourvish, Terence Richard
   Railways and the British economy, 1830–1914. –
   (Studies in economic and social history).
   1. Railroads – Great Britain – History
   2. Great Britain – Economic conditions
   I. Title II. Series
   385'.0941   HE3018

ISBN 0–333–28365–1

This book is sold subject to the standard conditions of the Net Book Agreement.

The paperback edition of this book is sold subject to the condition that it shall not, by way of trade or otherwise, be lent, resold, hired out, or otherwise circulated without the publisher's prior consent in any form of binding or cover other than that in which it is published and without a similar condition including this condition being imposed on the subsequent purchaser.

Contents

Acknowledgements	6
Note on References	6
Editor's Preface	7
1 Introduction: The Railways, a Victorian Industry	9
2 The Formative Years: 1830−70 (i) Investment	12
3 The Formative Years: 1830−70 (ii) Construction	20
4 The Formative Years: 1830−70 (iii) Operation	26
5 Railways and Economic Growth: 1830−70	33
6 The Mature Stage: 1870−1914 (i) Economic Performance	41
7 The Mature Stage: 1870−1914 (ii) Government and the Railways	49
8 Conclusion	57
Tabular Appendix	58
Notes and References	60
Select Bibliography	62
Index	67

Acknowledgements

I should like to thank Michael Miller for reading a first draft and making several useful criticisms, Roy Church and Ashok Parikh for their help with specific problems. Christopher Smout encouraged me at all stages and helped me lick the manuscript into shape. None, of course, is responsible for any imperfections that remain.

T. R. G.

Note on References

References in the text within square brackets relate to the items listed alphabetically in the Select Bibliography, followed, where necessary, by the page numbers in italics; for example [Reed, 1969: *8*]. Other references in the text, numbered consecutively throughout the book, relate to the Notes and References section.

Editor's Preface

SINCE 1968, when the Economic History Society and Macmillan published the first of the 'Studies in Economic and Social History', the series has established itself as a major teaching tool in universities, colleges and schools, and as a familiar landmark in serious bookshops throughout the country. A great deal of the credit for this must go to the wise leadership of its first editor, Professor M. W. Flinn, who retired at the end of 1977. The books tend to be bigger now than they were originally, and inevitably more expensive; but they have continued to provide information in modest compass at a reasonable price by the standards of modern academic publication.

There is no intention of departing from the principles of the first decade. Each book aims to survey findings and discussion in an important field of economic or social history that has been the subject of recent lively debate. It is meant as an introduction for readers who are not themselves professional researchers but who want to know what the discussion is all about – students, teachers and others generally interested in the subject. The authors, rather than either taking a strongly partisan line or suppressing their own critical faculties, set out the arguments and the problems as fairly as they can, and attempt a critical summary and explanation of them from their own judgement. The discipline now embraces so wide a field in the study of the human past that it would be inappropriate for each book to follow an identical plan, but all volumes will normally contain an extensive descriptive bibliography.

The series is not meant to provide all the answers but to help readers to see the problems clearly enough to form their own conclusions. We shall never agree in history, but the discipline will be well served if we know what we are disagreeing about, and why.

University of St Andrews   T. C. SMOUT
                                                          Editor

1 Introduction: The Railways, a Victorian Industry

WHILE the 'railway' has a long history, stretching back to ancient times, the railway in the modern sense was very much an innovation of the mid–late 1820s. The Stockton and Darlington (opened 1825) and the Liverpool and Manchester (opened 1830) combined the essential features – specialised track, mechanical traction, facilities for public traffic, and provision for passengers. And the industry was established in the next half-century or, more exactly, in a series of promotion 'manias' in the late 1830s, mid-1840s and mid-1860s. By 1875 over 70 per cent of the final route mileage had been constructed. Although historians have recently attempted to play down the economic effects of this new transport technology, there is no doubting its tremendous impact on Victorian society. Bringing a transformation in the speed and comfort of personal travel and a marked improvement in the reliability of freight movement all over the country, the railway inspired universal admiration. Charles Dickens, for example, amazed by his London–Paris journey in eleven hours in 1851, could only bless the South Eastern Railway for 'realising the Arabian Nights in these prose days'.[1]

The railways were also a considerable addition to the industrial structure. In their promotion and construction they represented the prime example of large-scale free-enterprise capitalism in nineteenth-century Britain and, as transport operators, were one of the largest industries. By 1875, the capital raised by United Kingdom companies had reached £630 million, equivalent to an annual rate of £12.5 million from 1825, considerably greater than the fixed capital formation of the 'giants' of the Industrial Revolution, such as cotton, coal, and iron and steel. Gross revenue was running at £52 million a year, 1870–5, equal to the value of wool output, and double that of coal, and employment on lines opened was 275,000 (1873), about 3 per cent of the occupied male labour force. In its maturity the industry attained even more impressive dimensions. By the end of 1913 raised capital, including nominal additions, exceeded £1330 million. In the same year revenue was almost £140 million gross, £51 million net, and employment stood at 643,000, or about 4.5 per cent of the United Kingdom's occupied males. Figures of this magnitude clearly place the railways among Britain's leading half-dozen industries.

The railways were further distinct in their high level of company concentration and developed management structures. Concentration was clearly visible at a comparatively early stage in the industry's development. The great 'mania' of 1845–7 left 15 large companies in control of 75 per cent of the United Kingdom's gross traffic revenue and 61 per cent of its paid-up capital in 1850. Two decades later, the same companies had 83 per cent of revenue and 80 per cent of capital, and it was possible to speak of a 'big four' – the London and North Western, Midland, Great Western, and North Eastern – sharing 44 and 38 per cent respectively. The position then stabilised, and the level of concentration in 1913 was essentially the same as in 1870.

It was these large trunk railways which proved to be, in Chandler's phrase, 'pioneers in modern corporate management'.[2] In 1850, for example, no less than 19 companies had raised capital in excess of £3 million, at a time when only a handful of industrial companies exceeded a capitalisation of £500,000. The special problems they encountered – joint costs, integrated processes, depreciation and obsolescence, heavy fixed investment, and a complex, diffuse organisation – all represented a tremendous challenge for inexperienced managements. Not surprisingly early operations were haphazard and uncertain. By the 1850s, however, a measure of progress was clear. While British industry in general was centred on the family firm or partnership, companies such as the London and North Western and, later, the North Eastern led the way in developing line and staff procedures, a delegation of authority to salaried managers, and a more comprehensive understanding of the complexities of accounting and costing in the modern business sense [Gourvish, 1972; Irving, 1976]. Financial crises and accounting uncertainties were not ruled out, of course, and management difficulties were not confined to the small or inexperienced companies. But the railways, in their search for answers to the problems of large-scale organisation and control, stimulated a more general development of the law and institutional framework surrounding joint-stock and limited-liability practice in Britain. 'The financial and commercial sides of railway development provided an example for an increasingly wide range of companies as the century progressed' [Reed, 1969:

8]. Finally the railways, with their potential for monopoly in inland transport, stimulated a far higher level of government control than existed in industries of comparable size [Parris, 1965]. Consequently the industry must be given a central place in any account of business organisation in the nineteenth century.

2 The Formative Years: 1830–70 (i) Investment

THE pattern of railway investment may be taken from three separate series: Mitchell's estimates of gross capital formation by United Kingdom railways, 1831–1919, which distinguish land purchase costs; Kenwood's series of *British* gross investment, 1825–75, which excludes land purchase, legal and parliamentary costs, but includes expenditure on repairs and renewals; and Hawke & Reed's raised capital data (that is, paid-up capital and loans) for the United Kingdom, 1825–1912 [Mitchell, 1964; Kenwood, 1965; Hawke & Reed, 1969]. While none of the series is ideal for all analytical purposes, they do agree as to the broad features of investment growth (Table 1). In the period to 1870,

Table 1
Railway Investment, 1825–69 (annual averages, £m.)

Period	Kenwood	Mitchell (including land)	Mitchell (excluding land)	Hawke & Reed
1825–9	0.25	—	—	0.28
1830–4	0.55	0.63*	0.53*	0.79
1835–9	4.69	6.52	5.62	6.44
1840–4	5.76	6.22	5.58	7.27
1845–9	20.03	29.02	25.18	31.02
1850–4	9.58	11.12	9.06	11.26
1855–9	10.02	9.82	8.56	9.86
1860–4	16.18	16.92	14.40	18.19
1865–9	18.94	19.24	15.06	18.64

* 1831–4

investment was very largely the story of three great 'waves' or 'manias', peaking in 1839/1840, 1847 and 1865/1866. The importance of this activity in the overall process of economic growth has not escaped attention. Mitchell, for example, has shown how rapidly the railways became a significant element in domestic investment, with gross capital formation (excluding land) consuming nearly 2 per cent of national income in the late 1830s. But it was in the 1840s that the order of magnitude shifted so dramatically. In Mitchell's now-familiar words, 'railway investment in the second half of the decade leapt ahead to great dominance, taking at its height in 1847 not far short of 7 per cent of national income . . . about two-thirds of the value of all domestic exports and half as much again as the value of cotton goods exported' [Mitchell, 1964: *322*]. In the years 1845–9 expenditure on railway construction (excluding land) averaged 4.5 per cent of Gross National Product (GNP) [Deane, 1968: *104*] and about 40–5 per cent of gross domestic fixed capital formation.[3] Total investment for *all* purposes took about 5.5 per cent of national income in the same period. With these levels, it is easy to accept Hawke's view that railway activity must have involved a reduction in consumption as well as a redirection of investment [Hawke, 1970: *210*].

We must not neglect the continuing importance of railway investment after the great 'mania'. After all, over 60 per cent of the capital raised between 1825 and 1875 came after 1850. Even in the relatively quiescent fifties expenditure (excluding land) amounted to 1.5 per cent of national income, not far short of the level in 1837–9. And the strength of the 1860s boom is quite clear. In the years 1862–6 railway investment (minus land) was equal to about 2.5 per cent of GNP and a third of domestic fixed capital formation [Deane, 1968: *104*; Feinstein, 1972: *T4*, *T85*].

Accepting that railway investment was sizeable, what part did it actually play in the growth process? Were the 'manias' merely a product of favourable market conditions, or did railway promotion lead economic growth? Here, there is now a broad consensus. The 25-year-old thesis of Matthews, echoed by Hughes and Mitchell, and supported with some reservations by Hawke, suggests that while railway promotion was an undoubted influence on general economic activity from the 1830s, its role was to support rather than to lead. Decisions to invest in railways were concentrated in the upswing of the cycle, and the lag between promotion and construction, extended by the nature of parliamentary procedures, meant that the contra-cyclical influence of railway-building was paramount [Matthews, 1954: *202f.*; Hughes, 1960: *184*, *206*; Mitchell, 1964: *329–30*; Hawke, 1970: *363–79*].

This hypothesis certainly holds true for the period before 1850. There is a clear lag between peaks of economic activity in 1836 and 1845 and peaks of railway investment in 1839–40 and 1847. Thereafter the relationship appears to weaken, however. Despite the plausible view that the capital market became an increasingly vital determinant of investment decisions, and the fact that the railways continued to search for capital primarily in boom periods, it is harder to find a clear lag in the 1860s and 1870s. Here we must recognise that the *exact* timing of the railway investment cycle is difficult to pin down with the existing estimates, and the possibility of fairly high margins of error in some years must not be discounted [Mitchell, 1964: *336*; Hawke, 1970: *199–203*]. Nevertheless, the contention that the railways played a sustaining role in the economy seems more fragile when applied to the period after the second 'mania', if timing is given a central place in the analysis.

Did factors endogenous to the railway industry influence the pattern of investment? Matthews has clearly indicated that the development of railway technology in the late 1820s and the commercial success of the Liverpool and Manchester Railway encouraged the promotional activity of the early 1830s, before the speculative stage in 1835–6. More contentiously the relative calm of 1838–43 is considered to have owed more to caution than to business stagnation [Matthews, 1954: *108–13*]. And if we accept that the speculative character of railway promotion has been much exaggerated, internally-generated factors must be given a more important place when assessing the impact of railway investment on economic fluctuations [Broadbridge, 1970: *168–75*]. Reed has taken the argument further. Referring to the period 1820–44, he suggests that railway development was essentially a 'rational' process, to be explained in terms of the geography of the system's expansion, technological factors (including significant shifts in costs in the early 1840s) and the resources available for railway building at various stages. Cyclical booms, he argues, did not induce the contemporaneous railway booms. The 'manias' emerged from pre-existing promotional booms, and these were largely the result of endogenous factors. The schemes of 1844, which are usually attributed to a revival of business confidence, or even to speculative fever, are here regarded as logical extensions to the network sponsored by the major companies [Reed, 1975: *1–31*].

Certainly endogenous factors were important. Besides technological change and commercial viability, alterations to parliamentary standing orders, making promotion more difficult from 1838 and easier again in 1842, acted on investment activity. Similarly Gladstone's Act of 1844, which referred to the possibility of a state purchase after 21 years of new companies earning 10 per cent net or more, helped to encourage over-optimism about the industry's future profitability during the second 'mania'. But the extent to which the existence of endogenous factors validates the hypothesis of railway development as a self-generating, 'rational' phenomenon must remain a matter for debate. Reed, while arguing that manias did not play a leading role to 1844, warned against the acceptance of a simple division between endogenous and exogenous variables, and referred to the co-existence of 'rationality' and risk in railway promotion. Thus while the timing of railway investment and the business cycle before 1850 suggests that boom conditions encouraged company promotion — and the importance of speculative elements in the investment of the late 1830s and mid-1840s must be admitted — the presence of endogenous factors does indicate that promotion was not only influenced by but itself influenced the prevailing economic climate.

Turning to the 1850s, Hughes has shown that the contra-cyclical role of railway construction continued. Investment lagged behind the peak of 1853 by one year, sustained the economy after the Crimean War (1856–7), and helped to induce recovery in 1858–9. However, the extent of these operations was much more limited than in the 1830s and 1840s. Indeed the railways' impact on trade cycle behaviour was greatly reduced after the second 'mania'. Lower profits deterred potential investors and increased the companies' dependence on favourable market conditions. The minor boom in promotion of the early 1850s was essentially a response to low interest rates, 1851–3 [Hughes, 1960: *184, 190–9*].

After 1860 investment fluctuations tended to coincide with those of the economy as a whole, with a peak in 1865–6, a trough in 1869, and a further peak in 1874–5. An explanation may be found in the maturity of the industry, and the slowing down of innovational elements. Much of the additional construction took the form of either ambitious and, on past experience, risky ventures in the London area, or extensions into the rural periphery of England, Scotland, and Ireland, where returns were expected to be lower than for the English main lines. Since profits remained well below the expectations of the 1840s, little was done to alter investors' caution. This, together with the diversion overseas of much speculative interest, drove home railways into the arms of contractors and finance companies, notably in the boom of 1863-5. These important intermediaries in the investment process were involved not only in floating new schemes but also in sustaining the financing of construction [Pollins, 1957: *41–51, 103–10*; Cottrell, 1976]. The fragility of many of these arrangements, however, helps to explain the rapid collapse of the boom in 1866. It does seem that the inability of the railways to generate investment without help explains the closer correspondence with the trade cycle and the reduction of contra-cyclical influence.

The railways' considerable investment activity aroused a great deal of contemporary criticism, with the fall in profits after 1846 and the capital waste induced by speculation being prime targets. However, many of the difficulties may be attributed to inexperience and the costs of pioneering development. High capital costs were established at an early stage: the United Kingdom average was as high as £33,000 per route-mile in 1844. Despite the 'excesses' of the second 'mania', the figure was only £5000 higher in 1875. Capital was undoubtedly wasted on projects which did not mature: of 9000 miles sanctioned between 1845 and 1848, only 5000 miles had been built by 1858. The amount lost was trivial, however, in the context of railway investment as a whole. And while increasing capitalisation helped to produce low rates of return for private investors after the second 'mania', there seems little doubt that *social* returns were more impressive. Hawke's calculations, while containing some controversial elements, suggest that net returns (net revenue *plus* social savings *minus* expenditure on capital works and rolling stock) for England and Wales were about 15–20 per cent from 1830 to 1870, with little deterioration after 1840 [Hawke, 1970: *405–8*]. If investors found the expectations of the early 1840s largely unfulfilled, the economy certainly gained from the investment process.

Railway investment also encouraged radical changes in the structure of the British capital market. The volume of railway business from the mid-1830s was such that the London Stock Exchange not only expanded but shifted its emphasis towards company securities. There was a rapid growth in investment journals, and provincial stock exchanges were created, in Liverpool and Manchester in 1836 and in Leeds, Glasgow and Edinburgh, among others, in 1844–5. These new institutions played a crucial role in mobilising local capital for railway purposes in the 1840s [Reed, 1969: *174–9*]. Such developments have impressed many historians. Indeed for Mitchell [1964] it was in the extension of the capital market and the encouragement to savings that railways had their most pronounced impact on the economy. The precise nature of their contribution must be clearly understood, however. Railways found their initial support outside the organised capital market, by obtaining promises to invest – subscriptions – at public meetings or through advertisement [Pollins, 1954]. And although local enthusiasm for railway schemes was always in evidence, the primacy of London and Lancashire mercantile interests in the promotion of companies is undoubted. Where railways made their impact, as Reed shows [1969], was in the subsequent market for railway paper (letters of allotment, scrip, partly-paid and fully-paid shares) that developed after the first promises to subscribe had been made. It was in the buying and selling of marketable securities that the railways extended the geographical and occupational base of investment, thereby transforming the Victorian capital market [Gourvish and Reed, 1971: *215*; Reed, 1975: *96*]. The speed with which the railways introduced a new class of investor to industrial capitalism should not be exaggerated, of course. The dominance of *rentier* investment – Clapham's 'blind capital, seeking its 5 per cent' – was not established until the general adoption of fixed-interest shares (preference and debenture) in the 1860s. Nevertheless, it is clear that one of the consequences of a relatively rapid turnover in shares was the steady extension of shareholding on a broad front.

Railway investors were protected by limited liability from the start, and it is logical to assume that the industry acted as a model for the companies which sprang up in the wake of the legislation of 1855–62. But should we go on to assert that 'It was the railways that won the acceptance of general limited liability' [Shannon, 1931, in Carus-Wilson, I, 1954: *376*]? Railway companies did not figure very much in the diverse public and parliamentary discussions about company liability in the early 1850s. If anything it was the criticisms they aroused, after the slump of the late 1840s and the downfall of George Hudson, that were used to good effect by *opponents* of limited liability [Jefferys, 1946, in Carus-Wilson, I,

1954: *347–8*; Saville, 1956: *425*]. Thus the direct links between the railways as a precedent and subsequent legislation may appear rather tenuous [Hawke, 1970: *390–2*]. However, the speculative 'mania' of the 1840s did stimulate a more general interest in the problems of financing business enterprise, and there is every reason to believe that the disillusionment with the railways' performance after 1850 was important in encouraging a search for safeguards to protect small capitalists on a general basis [Cf. Pollins, 1971: *44*]. While it would be foolish to argue that railways were the *only* motive force for changes in company law, the application of railway experience to a wider field should not be ruled out.

The difficulties experienced by railways had a positive influence in other areas too. The inability of companies to finance construction by share capital alone opened up the channels of investment to emerging institutions such as the joint-stock banks and the larger insurance companies. Between 1825 and 1844, no less than 37 per cent of the total capital raised for railways was in the form of loans and debentures – nearly £27 million – and institutions benefited greatly from the increased opportunities for lending. The industry's dependence on geared stocks was a clear example for companies facing investment problems in other sectors. The railways led the way in the use of preference shares and in the conversion of short-term debentures into perpetual debenture stock. By 1870 48 per cent of United Kingdom railway capital (excluding loans) was of the fixed-interest type.[4]

The difficulties of sustaining investment in railways, and especially in the more marginal concerns, also encouraged stockbrokers, bankers, and other intermediaries to play a more active role in railway management. Leading stockbroking firms, such as Foster & Braithwaite, Heseltine Powell, and Henry Cazenove, were never quite the passive agents Pollins [1954] makes them out to be [Reed, 1975: *87–8*]. They were frequently called in by companies to advise on the state of the money market, to help with the placing of capital, and to introduce individuals willing to lend on mortgage. By the 1870s they represented a formidable 'investment lobby', with the ability to exert considerable pressure on managerial policy [Gourvish, 1978: *190*]. While railways retained control of capital creation, it would be wrong to assume that there was no necessity for assistance in the form of underwriting of issues. The brief but crucial intervention of contractors and finance companies has already been mentioned. In the decade or so prior to the Overend, Gurney 'crash' of 1866, they kept several companies afloat. But bankers and brokers were also involved in underwriting. A notable example, the South Eastern Railway's conversion of a £4 million loan debt into a 5 per cent debenture stock in 1868, was managed by a capitalist syndicate which included Harman Grisewood, the London stockbroker, and prominent bankers such as George Carr Glyn and Henry Rawson.[5] Thus the long-term growth of railway investment helped to expand the horizons of financial institutions and involve them more closely in the problems of industrial enterprise.

3   The Formative Years: 1830−70
(ii) Construction

OVER forty years ago, Leland Jenks indicated the importance of distinguishing between the railway as 'a construction enterprise' and as 'a producer of transportation services' [in Carus-Wilson, III, 1962: *222*]. While it is not always easy to isolate the economic effects of railway enterprise in this way, there is no doubt that the 'construction phase' was a major activity in its own right. Despite the lack of complete data, it can be confidently asserted that before 1850 the employment generated by railway building dwarfed that created by railway operation (with the exception of 1843 and 1844), and that annual gross capital formation exceeded annual gross revenue (except in 1844). The early railway age, then, was essentially an age of construction. Between 1830 and 1870 about 30,000 miles of track were laid to form routes totalling 15,500 miles. The associated demand for men and materials − unskilled labour and iron products in particular − was large enough to merit a separate analysis.

Official information on labour employed is restricted to the years 1847 to 1860. But if we make use of the strong correlation between capital outlay on works and employment [demonstrated by Hawke, 1970: *ch. x*], we may derive adequate estimates from Mitchell's expenditure data [1964: *appendix, table 1*]. Thus over the period 1831−70 an average of 60,000 men were engaged annually in building railways, or about 1 per cent of the occupied male labour force.[6] This addition to total employment may not appear very dramatic in itself. However, attention must be concentrated on the short but crucial periods of hectic activity in the late forties and mid-sixties when the numbers employed were considerable. In 1845−9 and 1862−6 annual employment was about 172,000 and 106,000 respectively. A parliamentary return for 1 May 1847 − the peak year − showed that 6455 miles of line were being built by no fewer than 256,509 men, about 4 per cent of the male workforce. The construction booms produced sudden surges in the demand for labour, and especially for unskilled labourers, who made up 80−5 per cent of those recruited. The outcome, in the late forties, was a substantial boost to effective demand in the economy at a time of depression. The wages paid in 1847 must have amounted to at least £16 million, and for the period 1845–9 about £11 million, or 2 per cent of GNP. Quite clearly the multiplier effects of these payments helped to cushion the severity of the downturn in economic activity, bringing much-needed relief to a large group of rural workers.

In the mid-sixties constructional wage-costs were high once again, averaging £7 million or so between 1862 and 1866. But here the railways' demands coincided with the upswing, and employment fell away sharply after the 'crash' of 1866. Indeed the rapid run-down of the navvy gangs after each boom greatly lessened the benefits of railway construction in employment terms. By 1852, for example, the workforce had dwindled to under 36,000 and after the 1860s boom it was probably no more than 33,000 by 1870. Some labourers were retained by the large contractors, such as Thomas Brassey, who turned their attention to continental railways when British demand faltered. A few were taken onto the permanent operating staff of completed lines, while others may have saved enough to emigrate. Details are elusive. However, the data suggest that the vast majority of the huge labour force recruited in 1845–7 must have returned to the pool of under-employed, unskilled labour when the 'mania' subsided, and no doubt a similar fate befell several thousands after 1866. The long-term benefits of the attraction of labour to railway building were thus rather limited, especially after 1850. Of more lasting significance was the permanent employment offered by companies open for traffic, which exceeded 100,000 by 1856 and 200,000 by the late 1860s.

Railway construction brought with it both sudden and sizeable demands for professional expertise, much of which was retained when lines were completed. It is not too much to say that the industry played a key role in encouraging the growth of occupational professionalism based on specialised work. Engineering, law, accountancy and surveying all received an important stimulus. In engineering, construction problems were met by a small élite group of consulting engineers: men such as Robert Stephenson, Joseph Locke, and Isambard Kingdom Brunel. But more routine matters were handled by a rapidly expanding army of civil engineers, whose ranks increased four-fold between 1841 and 1851. Elsewhere it is difficult to distinguish between constructional and operational demands. However, it is clear that the 'construction phase' created lucrative opportunities for parliamentary agents specialising in private bill business and for solicitors handling company transactions, while the surveying profession was encouraged to leave its land-measuring traditions behind to concentrate on valuation and arbitration [Thompson, 1968]. Like the navvies, the professions were not immune from cut-backs once railway booms had subsided. The number of parliamentary agents, for example, which increased from 27 to 141 between 1841 and 1851 (England and Wales), fell back to 70 by 1861 [Reader, 1966: *163*]. However, the very concentration of the railways' demand for professional services had beneficial effects too. The urgent need for surveyors in the 1840s, for example, attracted a number of 'ruffians and rogues' into the occupation, emphasising the need for professional control and accelerating the process of specialisation and differentiation [Thompson, 1968: *14—15*].

There is general agreement that the construction of Britain's railways had its greatest impact in the backward-linkage effects on the iron industry. Wrought-iron rails were the major product purchased, but there was also a substantial demand for iron in chairs to fix the permanent way, bridges, miscellaneous equipment, locomotives, and rolling stock. Once again, however, the *long-term* significance of this additional demand has been challenged. Mitchell has estimated the pig-iron requirements of United Kingdom railways for their permanent way (rails, chairs, bridges, and so on) and concluded that while these were of paramount importance in the mid–late 1840s, particularly in terms of home demand, the same could not be said of the construction phase as a whole. Thus in the years 1844—51 about 18 per cent of United Kingdom pig-iron output went into permanent-way materials for United Kingdom companies, about 29 per cent of the pig iron used at home [Mitchell, 1964: *325*]. In 1848, the peak year, the percentages were as high as 30 and 40 respectively. But it is difficult to talk of 'dominance' after 1852. Exports grew steadily, and the railways' share of iron output fell back to under 10 per cent (8.2 per cent, 1852—69, according to Mitchell). The home-market share remained larger, but even this did not exceed 20 per cent after 1850. Moreover, the collapse of the 'manias' was a highly disruptive element for many iron companies, particularly in 1841—3, but also at the end of the decade. Hawke's conclusion is uncompromising. Railways, he asserts, 'were not essential to the existence of an iron industry . . . nor were they responsible for technical advances and external economies in the finishing processes and rolling mills' [1970: *245*]. Thus the diffusion of Neilson's hot-blast technique in the 1830s, and the surge in export growth after 1840, rather than domestic railway demand, are now stressed as the decisive influences shaping the expansion of the industry [Hyde, 1977].

Is this picture likely to remain unchallenged? First, we can scotch the notion that a more intensive statistical inquiry might lead to results of a vastly different order of magnitude. It is true that, in order to estimate railway demand, a large number of broad if not sweeping assumptions have to be applied to an inadequate data base [Cf. Vamplew, 1969: *34–5*]. And some of Mitchell's assumptions – in particular that of an average rail-life of 10 years – have been queried by Hawke [1970: *246–57*]. But Hawke can only conclude that Mitchell's estimates may err slightly on the generous side, and it is interesting to note that the subsequent studies of Hawke (England and Wales) and Vamplew (Scotland) broadly confirm his analysis. Thus for 1844–51 they suggest that the permanent-way requirements of British railways (excluding Ireland) consumed 15 per cent of United Kingdom pig-iron output and represented 24 per cent of the home market.[7]

But this is not the end of the argument. The analysis presented so far has been a partial one. We have by no means examined *all* the iron demanded by railways in their construction phase. Locomotives, rolling stock and equipment probably required an additional 20–5 per cent on top of permanent-way demand. Nor have we really begun to trace the *full* extent of the backward linkages from railways to iron, both direct and indirect, and embracing other industries such as coal and engineering. Equally the role of railway demand in helping to promote the industry's technological development deserves further study, particularly in the blast-furnace sector, where scale economies in association with the hot-blast may have been encouraged [Hawke, 1970: *241–2*; O'Brien, 1977: *65–7*]. These are all difficult areas to investigate, however, and some may lie beyond the historian's grasp. But we would do well to recognise that our present researches probably add up to an underestimate rather than an overestimate of the railways' influence.

One contribution has been accepted. Railway demand certainly induced the growth of iron production in particular regions. Foremost among these was south Wales. Hawke has been at some pains to show that Welsh ironmasters received more than a proportionate share of the orders for rails, particularly before 1850. The lack of quantified material is a serious handicap, however, and some of the railways he cites seem distinctly mysterious ('Brighton Croydon and Dover Street', 'Dover and Eastern Counties' [1970: *221*–*2*]). But the qualitative evidence is sufficient to support the contention that a great deal of the early demand for rails was supplied by south Wales, playing no small part in that region's growth. The industries in Cleveland and south Staffordshire also appear to have received a welcome stimulus from railway demand. In Scotland, however, there was certainly no dependence on the orders of Scottish railways [Vamplew, 1969]. But it would be illuminating to discover the extent to which this region was concerned in supplying the wider United Kingdom market.

Finally, there remains the important observation that in assessing the full effects of railway demand on the iron industry we should look at the wider market for railway materials. Export demand was in large measure a *railway* demand, and British ironmasters supplied large quantities of bar-iron and iron rails to the world market. If this is added to domestic demand, the dependence of the industry on railways is transformed. Fremdling [1977] has produced estimates which show that 26 per cent of pig-iron production went into railways in the years 1844–51, and 18 per cent in 1852–9. But these figures are surely too low. If we simply add the data for exported railway iron [Mitchell and Deane, 1962: *146*–*7* (assuming, for the period before 1855, that *all* bar-iron exports were railway exports)] to Mitchell's estimate of domestic demand, we find that the iron industry was dependent on railways for no less than 39 per cent of its output, 1844–51, and 24 per cent, 1852–69. A more informed estimate of total demand from 1856, when railway exports were first enumerated separately, to 1870, is 22 per cent [Riden, 1980: *T3.7*]. The relevance of all this to our present task is still a matter for discussion, of course. Mitchell and Hawke did not include exports in their analyses because they were concerned with the railways' *internally*-generated effects, and therefore Fremdling's claim to have corrected the 'misleading' impression left by Hawke is rather specious. Nevertheless, it is interesting to speculate whether exports of railway iron would have expanded so fast without the prior support of a successful domestic industry. To conclude, although domestic railways alone took under 10 per cent of pig-iron output between 1835 and 1869 and were clearly dominant for only a short time in the 1840s, the full importance of the 'construction phase' for the iron industry was probably greater than these figures by themselves suggest.

Steel rails began to replace iron in the 1860s. Some of the larger companies, such as the Midland, and London and North Western, led the way in experimentation, and as early as 1863 the latter acquired the right to use the Bessemer patent in its rolling mills at Crewe [Simmons, 1978: *148—9*; Gourvish, 1972: *241*]. But the industry as a whole was more cautious, given the price and uncertain quality of early Bessemer steel, and substitution was also sometimes delayed by close links with the iron companies [Irving, 1976: *132—4*]. It was not until the mid-1870s, outside our period, that there was a substantial shift to steel.

Railway construction stimulated demand for other products, notably coal, engineering products, timber and building materials. Unfortunately the evidence on these linkages is rather thin. In terms of total production, the railways' impact on the coal industry has been considered small. However, a very rough guess for the peak years 1844—51 suggests that as much as 6—10 per cent of coal output went into making iron for railway uses.[8] For engineering we have Mitchell's suggestion that about 20 per cent of the industry's output was in the form of railway rolling stock in the later 1830s and 1840s. But the more important observation is that railways in essence created a new sector — mechanical engineering [Mitchell, 1964: *327—8*]. Two principal effects arose from this. The concentration of production for the home market in the railway companies' own workshops not only had the effect of establishing important training grounds for engineers, but induced the independent rolling-stock producers to specialise almost entirely in overseas markets. Brick production also received a direct stimulus. It seems that about 25—30 per cent of total production went into railways in the 1840s [Mitchell, 1964: *328—9*; Hawke, 1970: *212n.*]. The industry's location may also have become more widely dispersed [Cf. Bagwell, 1974: *118*].

The importance of backward linkages cannot be equated merely with the proportion of total output consumed. But preliminary findings such as those above suggest that the linkages resulting from railway construction were far-reaching in a still maturing economy.

4 The Formative Years: 1830–70 (iii) Operation

RAILWAY traffic – both passenger and freight – grew steadily from the time reasonably reliable data were first collected (in the early 1840s).

Table 11
United Kingdom Railways: Traffic, 1842–75

year	passenger numbers (million)	traffic revenue (£m.)	freight tons (million)	traffic revenue (£m.)	total revenue (£m.)
1842	24.5	3.1	5.4	1.6	4.8
1846*	43.8	4.7	17.0†	2.8	7.6
1850	72.9	6.8	38.0†	6.4	13.2
1865	251.9	16.6	114.6	19.3	35.9
1875	507.0	25.7	199.6	33.3	61.3

Source: *Railway Returns*. To 1854, mails, parcels, etc, were counted as freight, thereafter as passenger traffic.
*Year ending 30 June for Great Britain, 31 Dec. for Ireland.
†Estimate.

Although some companies created new traffic, particularly in the coal-fields of north-east England and Scotland, the principal aim was to supply improved transport facilities for existing customers. The trunk-line railways which eventually dominated the industry established themselves by specialising in high-tariff business, taking high-fare-paying passengers from the stage coaches and high-value merchandise from the road carriers and, to a lesser extent, from canals and coastal shipping. Here, quite apart from price, the railway offered a speed and all-year-round reliability unmatched by its rivals, which were important considerations for affluent travellers and for manufacturers and traders anxious to relieve the burden of high inventory costs.

As the industry expanded, however, there were two significant changes in the composition of the business it handled. The first was an increased emphasis on freight from the mid-1840s. In the decade 1835–45 the major companies had concentrated on passenger traffic, deriving three-quarters of their gross revenue from this source. By 1850, however, the proportion had fallen below a half, and the preference for light merchandise traffic disappeared. The second change was a shift within passenger traffic to third-class. In 1845–6 third-class passengers made up under half of total numbers and produced only a fifth of total revenue. But by 1870 the proportions had risen to 65 and 44 per cent respectively [Gourvish, 1980]. An intensification of competition in the industry from the mid-1840s, encouraged by government policy, and the uninterrupted increase in the size of capital accounts, led traffic managers to pursue a larger-volume lower-margin business with considerable vigour.

Mitchell, echoing Clapham, plays down the market-widening effects of railway freight operations before the late 1840s. Railways, he suggests, were slow to exploit their advantages, a notable example being the failure to wrest a significant share of the London coal traffic from coastal shipping until the 1860s. It was only with the company amalgamations of the late forties and the improvement of traffic interchanges via the Railway Clearing House that railways were able to challenge the canals and extend the market [Mitchell, 1964: *319–20*]. Railways did not build up a large freight business until the 1850s, it is true, but the thesis of 'missed opportunities' is a rather misleading one. As late as 1835 locomotive technology was confined to a relatively few companies, and it was not until the early 1840s that locomotives were equal to the task of hauling heavy goods trains. Moreover, it was only in 1839 and 1840 that there was a clear recognition by government that railways should exclude private operators and monopolise the conveyance of traffic on their lines. At most then we are talking of a 'lag' of five years or so, and here managerial preference rather than constraints determined traffic emphasis. Amalgamations and the administration of the Railway Clearing House certainly facilitated long-distance freight flows, but the traffic was mainly short-distance in character, with the average distance travelled no more than 20–30 miles [Hawke, 1970: *64*]. Railway companies preferred high-value traffic where they were in a position to choose, and with profits in excess of 6 per cent to 1846 there was little to disturb this preference until the 'mania' brought its crop of duplicate lines and the escalation of capital expenditure. The London coal traffic, referred to by Mitchell, specially favoured coastal shipping: inland, railways quickly captured the coal business [Hawke, 1970: *169*]. The emphasis should therefore be placed on the *speed* with which railways took up low-margin freight (especially coal) once circumstances demanded it. Certainly the canals and navigations continued to provide valuable services to the economy into the 1850s. But their decline was swift once the railway companies accepted Mark Huish's dictum (1848) that 'quantity is the essential element of Railway success' [Gourvish, 1972: *135*].

The decision to pursue quantity was made at a time of falling profits. In the post-'mania' depression the ordinary dividends of the leading companies fell by half to below 3 per cent in 1850. Cyclical influences were present, of course, but the railways now faced a more permanent change in their operating environment, occasioned by the government's encouragement of competition on the one hand, and its insistence on more stringent controls on pricing freedom on the other. Nevertheless, the next 25 years witnessed a steady if modest improvement. The net rate of return on United Kingdom railway capital rose from 3.75 per cent in the mid-1850s to about 4.5 per cent in the early 1870s, by which time the ordinary dividends of the major companies were averaging 5–5.5 per cent.

For many historians this development is to be seen largely in terms of improved capacity utilisation. Railways were relatively under-used in 1850, and were able to increase traffic over the next two decades without additional heavy investment. Hawke, who estimated that total factor productivity (based on *net* capital) on the railways of England and Wales increased by 3 per cent a year (1840–70), attributed this growth almost entirely to improved capital utilisation, contending that the contribution of management, especially after 1850, was minimal [1970: *304–8*]. This assessment should not be accepted at face value, however. The productivity index is not immune from criticism, especially for the weight given to capital inputs [Engerman, 1971; McCloskey, 1971], and we should not neglect the possibility that the established companies did a great deal to lessen the adverse effects of the 'mania' and its operational aftermath. Traffic management was characterised by periods of cut-throat competition, but these tend to hide the substantial improvement in inter-company co-operation, as seen in the plethora of traffic-sharing agreements and the steady expansion of the Clearing House. Moreover, the shift in competitive emphasis from price to quality of service does not appear to have had a detrimental effect on labour productivity [Cf. Hawke, 1970: *311*]. Certainly railway management had its problems. There were particular difficulties with costing and pricing, and it is no surprise to learn that profit-maximisation was not energetically pursued [Hawke, 1969]. However, it does seem that the gradual recovery of profits after 1850 owed something at least to the ability of managers to conceive market strategies which were of necessity far removed from the selective incursions of the 1830s and early 1840s.

While there is general agreement that the railways stimulated an overall reduction in United Kingdom transport costs, both by introducing lower rates themselves and by forcing competitors to cut their own charges, the extent of the reductions, and the effects on markets and commodities, almost defy generalisation. The difficulty of establishing an 'average' price differential, with the aim of assessing the impact on the economy as a whole, is a very real one, as can readily be seen in Hawke's attempt to measure the social savings represented by railway services (see chapter 5). All we can do here is to point out the broad areas of change.

Jackman [1916: II, *605*, *635*; 1962 edn], referring to the period *c.* 1830–45, has ventured the guess that railways under-cut the road coaches by a modest amount, possibly 15–20 per cent, and the canals by a more substantial 30–50 per cent. However, it is difficult to accept his interpretation without reservation. In the passenger sector much depends on the nature of the comparison that is being made. On the major trunk routes, the railway companies soon swept away the coaches and were able to keep fares close to the maximum permitted by their private acts — about $3\frac{1}{2}d.$ per mile first-class and $2\frac{1}{2}d.$ per mile second. These charges were indeed only marginally lower than those previously charged for 'inside' and 'outside' coach travel. But most rail services were superior in speed and comfort to the best the coaches could offer. A fairer comparison is that between 'inside' coach travel at about $4d.$ per mile and *second*-class rail (at about $2-2\frac{1}{2}d.$): here the cost savings created by the railways were much more substantial than Jackman suggests.

Turning to freight, Jackman's proposition has the implicit

support of Hawke, who estimated the cost of non-rail transport to be 3*d.* per ton-mile, and accepted Lardner's figure of 1.67*d.* for the average rail tariff in the mid-1840s [Hawke, 1970: *64, 86*]. Certainly the evidence we have indicates that canals and coastal shipping companies frequently reduced their rates in anticipation of railway competition, and where railways intervened the result was invariably a sharp initial reduction in charges. When the railways first competed for the Aberdeen–London livestock traffic, for example, coastal shipping rates came down by 40–60 per cent [Channon, 1969]. There appears to be a general agreement that the railways encouraged a widespread reduction in costs before they themselves became substantial movers of freight. But given the lack of data, particularly for non-rail transport, and the complexities of the business – note the importance until the late 1840s of independent shippers dealing direct with the public – our confidence in specific percentage reductions must be limited.

The railways' search for larger traffic volumes after *c.* 1845 naturally had the effect of lowering their average rates. This can clearly be seen in the passenger department. The average fares of the major companies fell by as much as 30–40 per cent from the early 1840s to the late 1850s, and there was a further reduction (of about 10 per cent) to 1870. The trend was also downwards with freight, where low-tariff mineral traffic (mostly coal) became an increasingly dominant element. By 1870 it made up 60 per cent of total tonnage. The companies made strenuous efforts to maintain rate levels. They absorbed about a third of the canal network by 1865, and there was a great deal of both inter-modal and intra-modal collusion to establish equal rates. But coastal shipping remained a powerful competitor, frequently upsetting the most meticulous arrangements to stabilise or raise rates. Moreover, the competitive area was far from small: in 1872 a Select Committee stated that sea competition influenced some rates at no fewer than 60 per cent of all railways stations [Barker and Savage, 1974: *72*]. Hawke [1970: *62*] suggests that average rates fell to 1.21*d.* per ton-mile in 1865, 28 per cent lower than Lardner's estimate for 1843–8. While this, like all such estimates, rests on insecure foundations, it is probably not far short of the mark.

The traffic-maximising policies followed by the major railways after the mid-1840s certainly had the effect of eroding the importance of spatial imperfections in industrial competition. Retailing was transformed, and essentially new traffics were encouraged in perishable goods – meat, fish, fresh milk and vegetables. However, it is generally agreed that, with the basic industries already well-established in 1830, the railways could do little more than cement existing patterns of settlement and industrial location. The work of Dyos [1961] and Kellett [1969], by pointing out the relevance of patterns of land ownership, market activities and *all* forms of transport, has served to warn us against exaggerating the impact of railways in altering the character of the major cities. Nevertheless, railways did help to open up a number of new industrial sites, for example in south Wales (iron, anthracite), south Yorkshire and the north-east (coal), and Northamptonshire (iron-ore). The growth of Middlesborough and Barrow-in-Furness depended to a large extent on the existence of railway communication, and there are the examples of a direct stimulus to urbanisation in the 'railway towns' such as Crewe and New Swindon and the intra-urban development encouraged by works at Stratford (London) and Gorton (Manchester). The extension of services was accompanied by an improvement in communications at all levels, via the telegraph, postal services, and newspapers – all closely dependent on rail facilities. Faster and cheaper travel also stimulated the growth of leisure activities, particularly in the coastal resorts. The railway's influence on the economy was truly ubiquitous.

A caveat must be inserted here. We must not be impressed by the piling of example upon example without reference to the scale of activity involved. In some of the areas mentioned above, the railway's impact was more qualitative than quantitative before the 1870s. This was certainly true of the perishable-goods trade [Cf. Hawke, 1970; Perren, 1975; Atkins, 1978], while the holiday resorts did not really cater for a mass market until the later nineteenth century. On the other hand, we must beware of neglecting those items which defy precise quantification. The linkage effects produced by railways in their operational stage should be added to those attributed to construction in chapter 3, and the difficulty of abstracting them does not mean that they should be ignored. The stimulus given to employment and to the coal industry is a case in point. For example, in the peak years of railway building, 1844–51, the coal used to run rail services, about 1.4 million tons per year or 3–4.5 per cent of coal output, was close to half that needed to meet constructional demand. In the next major boom, 1862–6, operational needs had risen to 4 million tons per year or 4.5 per cent of coal output, exceeding the demand for constructional purposes (about 2.8 – 3.5 million).[9] And all this is quite apart from the implications of improved freight services for the wider market in coal.

The railway reduced the cost and greatly improved the quality and volume of Britain's transport. The economic effects were naturally diffuse, and some were not quantitatively impressive before 1870. However, the overall impact was such that the railways must be clearly associated with the shift of Britain's economy to a more sophisticated, mature stage.

5 Railways and Economic Growth: 1830—70

WHILE nineteenth-century commentators had little hesitation in assuming a direct relationship between the growth of the railway network and the pace of economic change, present-day historians are more cautious. Rostow's work has established that the railways cannot be associated with Britain's industrial 'take-off', which came in the late eighteenth century [Rostow, 1960]. This is not to deny them a role in the subsequent stage, the 'drive to maturity', where cost-reducing market-widening effects, the stimulus to exports, and the encouragement to expansion in coal, iron and engineering are all relevant. But Mitchell [1964], in the first critical review of the literature, concluded that even here the railways 'did not have a very great immediate impact', that is before c. 1850, except in relation to the capital market. Furthermore, claims that railways played a decisive role in raising investment levels have also come under fire recently. The commonly-held view that it was railway investment which lifted Britain's investment ratio above 10 per cent for the first time looks more fragile now that Feinstein has challenged Deane's estimates of capital formation and suggested that the significant leap came in the 1780s, despite the author's understandable doubts about the quality of his evidence [Feinstein, 1978]. Similarly the contention that railways rescued Britain from a serious investment crisis in the 1830s and 1840s — a 'crisis of capitalism' — has been roundly condemned as exaggerated [Church, 1971; 1975]. While intuitively we may feel that the railways were intimately if not crucially bound up in the growth process after 1830, we must begin with a more equivocal stance than was customary in the days of Clapham, when the period 1820—50 could quite simply be labelled 'The Early Railway Age'.

How much, then, did the railways really contribute to British economic growth between 1830 and 1870? Can this question be answered with any degree of confidence? A great deal now rests on our interpretation of the work of Hawke [1970] who, in applying the cliometric techniques of the American scholars Fogel [1964] and Fishlow [1965] to the railways of England and Wales, produced the most important single contribution of the last decade. Hawke, however, did not claim to be offering a comprehensive analysis of the impact of the railways on the economy. Instead he addressed himself to the more limited concerns of 'social saving theory', asking: 'To what extent did the economy depend on railways in 1865?', 'to what extent could the national income of 1865 have been attained without the innovation of railways?', and, more exactly, what would have been the cost of dispensing with railways and transporting passengers and goods by road and canal? The basic arithmetic is set out in Table III.

Hawke assumed that railway charges were equal to resource-costs, and compared the aggregate data with results derived from estimates of the resource-costs of 'non-rail' alternatives — coaches for passenger travel and canals for freight. Coastal shipping was excluded due to lack of evidence, and no account was taken of the railways' mail, parcels, luggage and other kinds of traffic, which in 1865 amounted to £1.5 million. For passenger traffic two calculations were made. The first, based on Lardner's comparison of classes, equated 'inside' coach travel with first-class rail, and 'outside' coach with second- and third-class rail [Lardner, 1850]. In fact, due to a calculating error (see Table III) Hawke uses figures which in effect compare first- and second-class with 'inside' and third-class with 'outside' fares. The second applied the formula of the Royal Commission on Railways of 1867, where posting was held to be equivalent to first-class, 'inside' coach to second, and 'outside' to third. Hawke favoured the latter as more appropriate for 1865, since the quality of service provided by railways in all classes was superior to anything that road transport could offer. But the choice has a significant effect on the size of the social saving: the comparison of posting at 2s. per mile with first-class at 2.11d. produces a saving of no less than £33.6 million — 5 per cent of the net national income of England and Wales. The total saving on passenger traffic, using the upper estimate, is over 7 per cent of national income.

In the case of freight, the initial comparison with the canals, where resource-costs were taken to be 2.3d. per ton-mile (not to be confused with canal *charges* estimated to be 3d.), revealed a relatively modest saving of £14 million. This was doubled, however, once allowance was made for livestock traffic excluded from the ton-mile calculation, extra wagon transport needed to take goods to canal locations, and inventory reductions. The final result is a saving on freight of about 4 per cent of national income. Hawke claimed that three-quarters of this – £21 million out of £25 – 8 million – came from savings in one category, the heavy mineral traffic, principally coal [1970: *178, 180*]. Railways certainly reduced costs here, but the importance of mineral savings is probably exaggerated by Hawke's comparison of the *actual* rates for railway minerals (0.6*d.* per ton-mile for coal, 0.8*d.* for other minerals) with *average* canal resource-costs at 2.3*d.* If Hawke's procedure is valid, the estimate of *overall* freight savings must surely be too low [O'Brien, 1977: *102 – 3*].

Hawke's conclusion, then, was that railway services in 1865 represented a social saving of between 7 and 11 per cent of the net national income of England and Wales, the variation depending on the degree of comfort passengers were prepared to sacrifice in the non-rail alternative. This 'interim' estimate later became a firm one after Hawke had investigated and largely discounted the possibility of additional savings from the railways' linkage effects (for example on labour and the iron industry) and external economies induced elsewhere (for example via pricing policies and through managerial, locational and investment stimuli).

Do Hawke's conclusions provide support for or against the view that railways were a vital element in Britain's growth process after 1830? Hawke implied a preference for the upper bound of 11 per cent for 1865, using it to conclude that 'the innovation of the railway . . . did have a considerable impact on the growth of [the] economy' [1970: *410*]. He was also impressed by the size of the net internal social rate of return on railway investment (social savings *plus* net railway revenue *minus* expenditure on reproducible capital), which he found to be 15 – 20 per cent for the period 1830 – 70. Thus while he recognised that social savings were much lower in earlier years – about 2.5 per cent of national income in 1850 and 6.5 per cent in 1855[10] – he implied that, in the 1860s at least, they were high.

Historians have not been eager to comment on the significance of Hawke's social saving figures. Church took them to demonstrate that 'the railways, as providers of transport services made a smaller contribution to the national economy than has been widely assumed' [1975: *31*]. O'Brien, on the other hand, has shown how it is possible to make the social saving ratio appear more impressive by considering the implications of making up the income sacrificed

Table III
Hawke's Social Saving Calculation for 1865

1 *Passenger traffic, England and Wales (2228.45 million passenger-miles):*

rail cost per passenger-mile	total rail cost	non-rail cost per passenger-mile	total non-rail cost	saving	saving as % net national income UK (£822 m.)	E. & W. (£666 m.)
1.35 d.	£12.5 m.	(1) 3.22 d.	£29.9 m.	£17.5 m.[a]	2.1[a]	2.6
		(2) 6.50 d.	£60.3 m.	£47.9 m.	5.8	7.2[b]

2 *Freight traffic, England and Wales (3120 million ton-miles):*

rail cost per ton-mile	total rail cost	non-rail cost per ton-mile	total non-rail cost	saving	saving as % net national income UK	E. & W.
1.21 d.	£15.7 m.	2.3 d.	£29.7 m.	£14.0 m.	1.7	2.1

3 Freight traffic – additional savings:

Livestock and meat traffic	£0.4–£2.5 m.
Supplementary wagon haulage	£10.6 m.
Inventory reductions	£0.0–£1.0 m.
Total (freight traffic):	£25.0–£28.1 m. 3.0–3.4 3.8–4.2[b]
Total (passenger and freight traffic):	
With passenger (1)	£42.5–45.6 m. 5.2–5.5 6.4–6.8
With passenger (2)	£72.9–76.0 m. 8.9–9.2 10.9–11.4

Source: Hawke [1970: *43, 48–9, 62, 88–9, 188*].

The non-rail cost figures are explained in the text below.

[a] Hawke [1970: *44*] gives the non-rail passenger cost (1) as £25.5 m., and the savings as £13.1 m., 1.6 per cent of United Kingdom national income (2.0 per cent of England and Wales national income). These are the correct figures, applying Lardner's formula. The figures above, which are incorporated in Hawke's subsequent calculations exaggerate the social saving (1) by £4.4 m or 0.6 per cent of England and Wales national income.
[b] Hawke [1970: *196*] refers to total passenger savings (2) as 'about 7.1 per cent' of England & Wales national income, and to freight savings as 'about 4.1 per cent'. His own arithmetic indicates percentages of 7.2 and 4.2, however, and these have been used here.

in 1865 over a 5 year period. For 1865–70 this would necessitate a 40 per cent increase in the growth rate, a similar increase in the gross investment rate, and a 5 per cent reduction in annual consumer expenditure [1977: 27–8]. Others have been less forthcoming, however. In two recent surveys of transport development, Hawke's figures were presented with little or no comment [Bagwell, 1974; Barker and Savage, 1974].

In fact the major obstacle to interpretation is the doubt as to whether Hawke's social saving estimates really mean very much at all. The weight of historical criticism has fallen on the methodological and empirical weaknesses which surround the calculations, many of which are inevitable given the slim data base available to the author. In terms of methodology, the social saving concept has obvious limitations, since it is a cost–benefit technique set in a partial equilibrium framework, and therefore more suited to the appraisal of individual projects than to the assessment of the impact of an entire industry over a long time-span. Most of the theoretical objections concern the validity of Hawke's *ceteris paribus* assumptions, for example, an inelasticity of demand for transport, and for quality of service in passenger travel, zero technical progress in the non-rail sectors, and constant real canal costs over time. This by no means exhausts the list of complaints, which clearly represents a real challenge to the practical usefulness of Hawke's work in helping us to reach a more precise measurement of the part played by railways in the growth process.

But even if we accept that, with all its inherent difficulties, the social saving approach has something to offer, there remain abundant criticisms of the way in which the estimates were constructed. For key calculations Hawke was frequently forced to rely on only one or two figures taken either from secondary sources, such as Lardner (whose estimates are for the UK, not England and Wales), or from evidence given to parliamentary select committees. Since the estimates of passenger-mileage, freight ton-mileage and, above all, non-rail resource-costs are affected, confidence in the end result must necessarily be limited. Particular attention has been directed at the fragility of the figure for canal costs, 2.3d. per ton-mile. This is made up, firstly, of 0.4d. for direct canal costs, derived from data for only two canals, the Leeds and Liverpool (1820–40) and the Kennet and Avon (1812–24), both of which lay outside the major traffic route from London to the north-west. Secondly, 1.5*d*. is added for shipping costs, on the slimmest of evidence, and a further 0.4*d*. on the grounds that canal journeys were 20 per cent longer than those by rail, a contention that ignores road haulage to railway stations. Equally numerous objections may be raised in all areas of the social saving calculation summarised in Table III (see, *inter alia*, Engerman, 1971; McCloskey, 1971; Saul, 1971; Aldcroft, 1972; Floud, 1972; and O'Brien, 1977].

As an illustration of the difficulties of interpretation, the Tabular Appendix (see below, pp. 58—9) indicates some of the opportunities for adjusting Hawke's social saving figure of 11 per cent on the basis of criticisms it has attracted. Without challenging his theoretical base or resorting to extravagant flights of fancy, it is possible to produce both a low saving of 2.66 per cent (Table I) and a high saving of 23 per cent (Table II). Neither of these is to be seen as a preferred alternative, but they clearly support the contention that Hawke's calculation is frail and therefore difficult to use in a broad context. In fact his was not the first attempt to provide a social saving figure for Britain's railways. A century before Fogel and Hawke, Dudley Baxter offered a simple 'back-of-envelope' estimate of the saving produced by cheaper rail services in the United Kingdom. 'Had the railway traffic of 1865 been conveyed by canal and road at the pre-railway rates', he conjectured, 'it would have cost three times as much' [Baxter, 1866, in Carus-Wilson, III, 1962: *41*]. In this way he obtained a saving of £72 million, about 9 per cent of net national income. Cynics may be forgiven for treating the calculations of both Baxter and Hawke with equal reserve, despite the disparity in sophistication. Thus while Hawke's work is undoubtedly a serious attempt to measure the strength of the railways' impact as an innovation, his calculations are more a frustration than an encouragement. As O'Brien has noted: 'Estimates of social savings . . . can only be used to make rather limited points in discussions of the relationship between railways and economic growth' [1977: *39*].

Hawke has much more to offer at the disaggregate level, as we have seen in earlier chapters. Building on Mitchell's pioneering essay he helped to deflate some of the more extravagant claims made for railways, for example in their impact on the iron industry and the labour market. More controversially, he challenged the extent of their contribution in areas such as business management and the capital market. Clearly many influences do not easily lend themselves to precise measurement, and the pitfalls in attempting to quantify variables should never be underestimated [Cf. Vamplew, 1971]. But critics have drawn up a long list of items for further study, ranging from engineering to retail trading, general communications to business skills, technological change to industrial location, and even in well-researched areas such as iron it would be rash to claim that the debate has now closed. Hawke's assessment of the ramifications of the railways' influence, particularly in terms of 'externalities', does seem to be unduly restricted. It is possible that further research will establish a firmer picture of the strength of the railways' linkage effects, especially where both constructional and operational stimuli are considered.

Railways did not occupy a central place in Britain's early industrialisation, of course, and references to their 'indispensability' for further growth in the mid-nineteenth century are to be ignored. But it is generally accepted that their impact was greater than that of any other single innovation in the period, and although a satisfactory measure of their contribution to the economy must necessarily remain elusive, this is not to imply that it was in any way a meagre one.

6 The Mature Stage: 1870–1914 (i) Economic Performance

BY 1870 the essential features of the railway industry – the basic network, organisational structure, and traffic patterns – had been established. But maturity did not mean stagnation. From 1870–1914 there was a four-fold increase in the number of passengers and a three-fold increase in freight tonnage. Route-mileage increased by 50 per cent, capital by 150 per cent, and gross revenue by nearly 200 per cent (Table IV). In fact inland transport was essentially rail transport in the late nineteenth century, although this is not to ignore the important role of road transport, and especially road haulage, as a short-haul feeder [Turnbull, 1979: 124–5]. But there can be no doubt that the contribution of the railways to the economy was much greater than in the mid-1860s. If Hawke had produced a social saving calculation for 1890, for example, it would have been two or three times greater than for 1865, amounting to 25–30 per cent of national income[11] (although note the criticisms of the procedure expressed in chapter 5). This is without making adjustments for areas in which the railway presence intensified after 1870, such as ancillary undertakings (docks, steamships and so on), the perishable goods trade, and the transfer of managerial resources to other sectors [Gourvish, 1973; 1979(b)]. However, historians have not been concerned with measuring the extent of this contribution to the late-nineteenth-century economy. Instead they have directed their attention to the declining profitability of the industry and its relevance to the wider debate about British retardation and weakening competitiveness after 1870. Railways have been regarded not only as a prime example of weakness in maturity but also, in their relationship with the coal industry, as a classic case of the inhibiting effects of related investment – the 'drag of inter-relatedness' [Frankel, 1955; Kindleberger, 1961]. Leaving aside the validity of such arguments – the latter in particular has been much debated – it is clearly important to establish at the outset the nature of the railways' performance in conventional business terms.

Table IV
The Growth and Performance of UK Railways, 1870–1912

year	route-miles	capital raised* (£m.)	gross revenue (£m.)	period	gross %	rate of return on capital net %		operating ratio
1870	15,537	529.9	45.1	1870–4	9.27		4.55	51
1875	16,658	630.2	61.3	1875–9	9.21		4.30	53
1880	17,933	728.3	65.5	1880–4	8.96		4.29	52
1885	19,169	815.9	69.6	1885–9	8.51	†	4.06	†	52
1890	20,073	897.5	79.9	1890–4	8.67	9.36	3.86	4.16	56
1895	21,174	1001.1	85.9	1895–9	8.65	9.97	3.71	4.27	57
1900	21,855	1176.0	104.8	1900–4	8.93	10.58	3.38	4.01	62
1905	22,847	1272.6	113.5	1905–9	9.14	10.77	3.42	4.03	63
1910	23,387	1318.5	123.9	1910–12	9.55	11.22	3.60	4.23	62
1912	23,441	1335.0	128.6						

Source: *Railway Returns*, P.P. 1913, Cd. 6954.
* Includes nominal additions to capital (£57m. in 1890, rising to £198.5m. in 1912).
† Rates of return using capital raised *net* of nominal additions to capital.

Unfortunately the basic difficulty remains that of establishing suitable tests of 'performance'. While there is a comparative abundance of statistical material on the companies, particularly after the Regulation of Railways Act of 1868, it is frustrating to find that we lack the most appropriate measures of efficiency — ton-miles, passenger-miles, and employment data. Without these, satisfactory estimates of productivity are difficult if not impossible to construct [Vamplew, 1971], and the limitations of studies based on rates of return, operating ratios and train-mile statistics must be fully recognised.

With this caveat firmly in mind, let us consider Table IV, which presents in its right-hand columns the three most commonly-used indicators of railway performance: the gross rate of return on capital raised; the net return; and the operating ratio, that is working costs expressed as a percentage of gross revenue. In all three series a deterioration is evident, although in no case was there a continuously falling trend over the whole of the period. The gross rate of return, a rough indicator of capitalisation, fell from 9.27 per cent in 1870–4 to 8.51 per cent in 1885–9, but then recovered to reach a level of 9.55 per cent by 1910–12. Returns would have been higher still (for example 11.22 per cent in 1910–12) had not the companies added nearly £200 million of nominal capital to their accounts in order to lower interest rates. However, the most important observation here is that returns were always higher than the 7.5–8.0 per cent of 1855–70, which suggests that if the railways were over-capitalised, it was not a problem introduced after 1870, as Aldcroft [1968(b): *12*] has claimed [Irving, 1978].

The net rate of return fell steadily from 4.55 per cent in 1870–4 to 3.38 per cent in 1900–4. However, it was not until the 1890s that returns fell below the 4.0 per cent level of the 1860s, and there was a minor recovery from 1901 to 3.6 per cent by 1910–12. Furthermore, the aggregate data exaggerate the fall in the return on capital actually raised for railway purposes. If we exclude the nominal, paper additions to capital, which can be distinguished from 1890, the 'deterioration' is slight. Net returns, while a little lower than in the 1870s, were always above 4.0 per cent. The operating ratio, on the other hand, certainly became worse. It went above 50 for the first time in 1873, above 55 in 1892, and above 60 in 1900. Nevertheless, even here there were alternate periods of rise and stabilisation. Overall, the statistics do not

43

suggest that the period 1870–1914 was one of steady deterioration. However, we may conclude that after two decades of recovery, 1850–70, the industry's earning-power fell back to the level of the early 1860s, and that operating margins narrowed significantly.

How are we to explain these developments? Ashworth [1960: 119–26] suggests that the railways were very largely the victims of the increased demand for transport. Traffic growth occurred mainly in the low-margin sectors – third-class passengers and small consignments of short-haul bulk freight – and with existing facilities stretched by the mid-1870s a large additional capital expenditure was necessary to provide the extra capacity. Nor could this new business be refused. The companies 'were in too vulnerable a position, competitively and politically, for them to risk turning away additional traffic or even to neglect the improvement of services in order to attract it' [Ibid., *121*]. The crucial factors in the industry's fortunes, then, were the level of competition and the pricing and service policies enforced by government and transport pressure groups.

To a great extent this thesis has been confirmed by subsequent research. The only significant dissentient is Aldcroft [1968(a); 1968(b)]. He accepts that the industry faced 'structural rigidities' in the form of inter-related industrial investment, traders' service demands, the small-load nature of much freight traffic, and government interference with the freedom to charge. But his main emphasis falls upon the weak response of railway management. The companies are strongly criticised for having incurred a vast expenditure on branch-lines and duplicate facilities without adequate reference to the likely rate of return, and for accepting a considerable element of cross-subsidisation in their services. Pricing was rarely related to operating costs, and little or no attempt was made to offset rising costs by improving traffic handling methods. These deficiencies are attributed to the empire-building mentality of railway leaders, which prolonged the industry's obsession with construction at the expense of operating efficiency.

The stress on faulty management has failed to command support, however. As we have seen, the industry's capital burden while certainly heavy did not become worse after 1870. Project appraisal was inadequately developed in most companies, it is true, and there were notable examples of unrealistic investment. The most glaring of these was the Manchester Sheffield and Lincolnshire's extension to London in the 1890s, inspired by the notorious 'empire-builder', Sir Edward Watkin. But detailed research reveals that both Watkin and his arch-rival, James Staats Forbes, pursued investment policies which accommodated network expansion at the expense of quality of service and so kept their companies' capital growth in step with that of the United Kingdom as a whole. Indeed many of their 'disastrous' lines were relatively cheap to build. The four most-criticised extensions of Watkin's South Eastern, for example, consumed only 10 per cent of the £8 million spent between 1872 and 1898 [Gourvish, 1978: *192*]. And in England and Wales only a very small proportion — about 5 per cent — of the capital spent between 1870 and 1900 went into unprofitable new companies.[12] By far the greater part of capital additions was devoted to essential improvements to the capacity and standards, including safety, of the main lines, particularly in the crowded urban areas, rather than to unprofitable ventures in sparsely populated districts. Some of this expenditure might have been avoided, of course, and the companies probably rushed into projects too enthusiastically in the late 1890s on the basis of temporary high profits and low interest rates [Cain, 1972: *626–7*]. But, in general, misplaced investment strategies were *not* the major cause of diminishing returns [Irving, 1976: *277*].

It is clear that we must focus our attention on the industry's operating problems. But, in doing so, it is important to recognise that the years 1870–1914 should not be taken as a whole. There were four distinct periods affecting the working environment, and these corresponded broadly with changing price trends. First, there was a sharp rise in costs in the early 1870s, which drove the operating ratio above 50. The ratio then stabilised between 1873 and 1890, since both revenue and costs per train-mile fell. The additional costs of an improved quality of service were offset by the falling price of materials (especially coal). However, in the 1890s, and notably between 1896 and 1901, there was a further more serious escalation in costs. The operating ratio rose above 60, thereby occasioning the contemporary criticisms of the industry [for example Paish, 1902] noted by Aldcroft. After 1900 the situation changed again. The operating ratio stabilised at a time of rising prices, and there was a substantial improvement in operating efficiency [Pollins, 1971: *91–100*]. Almost all of this occurred in the freight department, where revenue per train-mile increased by no less than 42 per cent, 1900–12 [Irving, 1978: 61].

At what stage were the operating weaknesses of the industry apparent? Pollins [1971] has suggested that the railways' difficulties were essentially problems of the late 1890s, and that these were palliated, to some extent, by an immediate efficiency drive. Certainly the period 1896–1901 was a challenging one. Operating costs increased sharply, traffic growth slowed down, and the extra burdens of newly-raised capital put pressure on profit levels. All this was accompanied by legislation seeking to control two key areas of railway economy – charges and labour costs. The Railway Regulation Act of 1893, which aimed to restrict excessive working hours, and the Railway and Canal Traffic Act of 1894, which in effect established the rates of 1892 as new maximum charges, were potent examples of the many efforts to make the railways conform to public expectations. Indeed, the virtual freeze on rate increases, confirmed by the judgment in *Smith and Forrest* v. *London and North Western &c.* of 1899, was the most important factor encouraging more efficient working after 1900 [Cain, 1972; 1978].

But it is easy to place too much emphasis on the adverse effects of changing price trends and government intervention from the mid-nineties. The diminishing returns experienced by the railways were a reflection of operating policies which had been established much earlier, that is in the mid-1870s and 1880s. Their effects were masked, however, by the fall in prices, which was sufficiently pronounced to leave the operating ratio, the contemporary measure of efficiency, in a stationary position. Thus the more important observation is not that the ratio was stable, but that it was stabilised at a level higher than that of the period 1850–72. The sharp rise in railway costs between 1872 and 1874 was not reversed. Instead, better services for lower- and lower-margin business required a considerable labour input, and with wages relatively 'sticky', it was the rise in labour costs, partly hidden by deflation, which was the root cause of the industry's operating difficulties. Although these were not fully exposed until the 1890s, the 1880s were the crucial decade. Traffic expanded, and the price of materials continued to fall, but the companies were unable to improve their traffic-handling efficiency in order to counteract falling charges and the rising cost of services [Irving, 1976; 1978].

How far were the companies to blame for this situation? Aldcroft, as we have seen, makes much of the industry's managerial shortcomings. Irving, on the other hand, while accepting that operating methods were 'inappropriate', suggests that these were largely influenced by the more hostile political environment in which the railways were placed after 1870. Directors and managers, it appears, were aware of the need to fill trains and prune uneconomic services, but they yielded to the demands of both passenger and trader in an attempt to ward off the possibility of further encroachment on their commercial freedom.

We are not suggesting that railway managements should be freed of all responsibility for their position after 1870. Much of Irving's work, for example, is based on the records of the North Eastern, an exemplar of advanced management practice, and he may well have ascribed too much to 'political pressure' and too little to the railways' failure to grapple with their internal weaknesses. The fact that 'worst-practice' lines, such as Watkin's South Eastern and Forbes's London Chatham and Dover, which specialised in passenger services, were able to effect economies by squeezing labour and curbing the quality of service [Gourvish, 1978: *196–8*] raises the possibility, at least, that other companies had more scope for manoeuvre than has been suggested. This is important in view of the intensifying and (after 1900) unrelieved problems with the passenger side of the railways' business, and the fact that these problems were recognised inside the industry [Cf. Findlay, 1889: *ch*. XV].

Weaknesses may also be found elsewhere. Cain is particularly critical of the railways' attempt to circumvent the maximum rates proposals of the early 1890s (drawn up under the Railway and Canal Traffic Act of 1888). The companies' 'shortsighted greed and clumsy diplomacy' did much to alienate public opinion, precipitating the less flexible Act of 1894 [Cain, 1973: *79–80*]. Finally recovery after 1900, achieved by freight economies and a greater measure of inter-company co-operation, might have been less impressive had the companies been able to raise capital on more favourable terms [Irving, 1971].

Nevertheless, the constraints imposed by a business community increasingly anxious about foreign competition and 'import preference' and eager to force railways into a 'public service' mould, and by governments legislating on passenger fares and safety in the 'public interest' added up to a very serious challenge to commercial freedom. Evidence of a significant change in attitudes after 1870 is abundant. As a Berwick trader bluntly put it (*c.* 1890):

'What we want is to have our fish carried at *half* present rates. We don't care a —— whether it pays the railways or not. Railways ought to be made to carry for the good of the country, or they should be taken over by the Government'.[13] The Railway and Canal Traffic Act of 1873, the Cheap Trains Act of 1883, and the legislation of 1888–94 were all part of a significant shift in public opinion. Railways were seen more as public corporations than as profit-making businesses [Alderman, 1973], and the companies responded to this change all too readily. It was in this environment that railways experienced diminishing returns, while producing substantial benefits for society as a whole.

7 The Mature Stage: 1870—1914 (ii) Government and the Railways

IN the United Kingdom the creation of the early railway network, from the choice of routes and the raising of capital to the operation of services, was left to private enterprise. The sole restraint on the free market was imposed by the private act procedure of Parliament, which required each new project to pass the scrutiny of committees of both Houses before obtaining powers to purchase land, and raise capital under conditions of limited liability. These acts, like those for the canals, contained clauses stipulating the size of the capital and fixing maximum charges or tolls for the use of the 'way'. Competition, it was hoped, would protect consumers from the threat of monopoly.

British policy was in sharp contrast with that followed in continental Europe, where the state's presence at all stages — planning, construction, and operation — was readily apparent. Critics such as Thomas Gray and John Morrison were quick to point to unfavourable comparisons, in particular the higher cost of construction in Britain [Gourvish, 1972: 23]. It soon became clear that additional controls were necessary. As early as 1839 a Select Committee accepted that the railways could not be operated like the canals, with individual carriers free to run their own trains on the payment of tolls. The companies had to be given a monopoly of train movement, and this raised fears of abuse, fears which were strengthened in the 1840s by the high-fares policy of the trunk-line companies and the first important amalgamations, which produced the Midland (1844) and London and North Western (1846) companies.

But as railways passed from the construction to the operating stage, governments wavered between advocating control and allowing the industry commercial freedom. Thus while some important precedents for state intervention were established in the period 1840—70, there were no firm or consistent guidelines, and supervision was general and exhortative rather than mandatory. The Government, it is true, created a supervisory body — the Railway Department of the Board of Trade — as early as 1840, with powers to inspect newly-constructed lines and receive accident reports. But the inconsistency of policy can be seen in the subsequent experiments with regulation — Dalhousie's Railway Board of 1844—5, a short-lived attempt to direct promotion during the second 'mania', and the independent but weak Railway Commissioners of 1846—51. The return to a Railway Department produced a more durable but scarcely more effective body. While we should not underestimate the cumulative contribution to improved safety of the inspectors' reports, the Department itself lacked effective powers and rarely acted to enforce its decisions, even where abuses were evident [Parris, 1965: *149—51, 200—1*].

Parliament's efforts were no more successful elsewhere. Gladstone's bill of 1844 was undoubtedly a serious challenge to the industry's independence, but it emerged in much-truncated form as legislation. The Act did impose the first important service obligation on the companies, that of operating a daily passenger train at fares of 1*d.* per mile. But the state-purchase clause was very much a watered-down affair, providing an option to purchase new companies after 21 years, and to reduce charges if net earnings amounted to 10 per cent or more. This was a remote possibility, particularly after the 'mania'. Ineffective regulation was also evident in the government's attempts to check the tendency towards company concentration and to deal with that *bête noire* of the trading community, preferential rates. Amalgamations were to be discouraged after Cardwell's Select Committee of 1852—3 had deliberated. But the North Eastern was sanctioned in 1854, the Great Eastern in 1862, and no less than 187 acts provided for company mergers in the 1860s [Dyos and Aldcroft, 1969: *164*]. Two of the giants, the London and North Western and Great Western, together absorbed 52 separate concerns between 1850 and 1875.

In its attitude to rates Parliament did make some progress. Despite the collapse of the policy of 'equivalents' (competition or lower charges), which had been pursued briefly by Dalhousie's Board, the maximum rates inserted in private acts were generally lower after 1845. In addition, steps were taken to curb 'undue preference' by establishing the principle of equal charging under equal circumstances (in the Railway Clauses Consolidation Act of 1845 and the Railway and Canal Traffic Act of 1854). However, equality was in practice difficult to enforce given the immense complexity of rates structures and the exclusion of 'terminal' charges — collection, delivery and so on — from consideration. Three decades of state intervention did more to facilitate railway development than to restrict commercial freedom. 'Parliament . . . proceeded upon the principle of not attempting to direct the active operations of railway companies or to give the Government, either directly or indirectly, any control over the safe or efficient working of the railways' [Wilson, 1925: *10*].

Parris sees the year 1867 as a major turning-point in the relations between government and the railways. Although the Royal Commission on Railways of 1865, which reported in that year, recommended no fundamental change of policy, it was followed by the Regulation of Railways Act of 1868 which introduced new elements of compulsion: a standard form of accounts, and the first interference in train working, a communication cord for passenger trains. This heralded a new period of intervention, which was stimulated by the return to more organised party government in Westminster. However, parliamentary activity continued to be characterised by an *ad hoc* response to problems, and there was no sharp break around 1870 in the legislative sense. A renewed concern about company amalgamations did lead to another Select Committee (1872) and the rejection of important merger proposals, including that of the London and North Western and the Lancashire and Yorkshire companies. It also produced, via the Railway and Canal Traffic Act of 1873, a new body, the quasi-judicial Railway Commission, whose function was to consider public complaints about rates and facilities. But the machinery was essentially *ad hoc* — the Commission had to be formally renewed each year after 1878 — and it needed a further select committee on rates in 1881 and a great deal of lobbying by farmers, traders, and industrialists before Parliament really tackled the rates question. It was not until the Railway and Canal Traffic Act of 1888 that the Commission — rechristened the Railway and Canal Commission — was made permanent and the railway companies were required to present revised schedules of rates.

The situation was similar in the field of railway safety. Governmental concern was evident in the early seventies as the pressure of increased traffic on existing capacity brought a higher rate of accidents, probably the worst in British railway history. The number of passenger fatalities in train accidents increased from 15 a year in the 1850s to 43 a year, 1870—4 [Wilson, 1925: *26—7*]. This prompted a closer supervision by the Board of Trade of company progress in introducing safety equipment – block signalling, the interlocking of points and signals, and continuous automatic brakes (Acts of 1871, 1873 and 1878). But Parliament was still reluctant to coerce the companies, its attitude no doubt influenced by experience with the communication cord, where a patently unsatisfactory method had been insisted upon in 1868 only to be withdrawn five years later. It required the emotive appeal of the Armagh accident of 1889, in which 80 people died, before a Railway Regulation Act made the principal safety devices compulsory.

But before we are led to the view that the railways' difficulties were delayed until the 1890s – a thesis we have examined earlier (chapter 6) – it must be recognised that outside the bare framework of legislation a change of mood was evident from the late 1860s. It is clear, for example, that amalgamations were inhibited by the threat of more severe restrictions on maximum charges. The proposed merger of the London Brighton and South Coast, South Eastern, and London Chatham and Dover in 1868 foundered in the Lords when the South Eastern refused to accept lower maxima as a condition of parliamentary approval, and by 1885 Laing, the Brighton's chairman, was quite certain that Parliament's attitude was such as to render 'anything like a fusion of interests . . . altogether impracticable'.[14] The effects of the safety legislation of the 1870s should not be underestimated. Voluntary progress by the companies was considerable. Between 1873 and 1889 the amount of United Kingdom double-track (passenger lines) worked by the absolute block increased from 42 to 95 per cent, while the percentage of locations with interlocking rose from 39 to 91. In 1878 only 18 per cent of locomotives and carriages were fitted with continuous brakes, but by 1889 the proportion was 92 per cent, with 73 per cent using approved automatic systems.[15] There was also the interference with traffic management of the Cheap Trains Act (1883), which made remission of passenger duty on fares of 1d. per mile and below conditional upon the provisions of adequate cheap travel for workmen. All this added up to a more hostile environment for railway companies, and one to which they proved sensitive. Their response in improving the quality of their services in an attempt to diffuse the pressure building up around them undoubtedly contributed to the lower margins and reduced profits of the latter part of the century.

The industry's freedom of action was even more restricted from the 1890s. Not only was there a virtual freeze on rate increases with the Act of 1894 (see chapter 6), but the government also turned its attention to a major element of railway costs — labour. Its concern originated in the Board of Trade's insistence that the long hours worked by railwaymen were an important cause of accidents. Certainly the extent of staff casualties was shocking, even by contemporary standards. In 1874–6, for example, 742 men were killed and at least 3500 injured each year, out of a total at risk of under 200,000. And although the accident-rate fell in relation to train-mileage as safety measures were introduced, it was still high in the early 1890s. The annual average for 1890–2 was 505 killed and 3040 injured, half of the incidents occurring in shunting operations. The government's response was to introduce machinery to curb 'excessive' working hours, make the industry follow the general scheme for compensating workmen, and give the Board of Trade further powers to order safety improvements (Acts of 1893, 1897 and 1900). As a result, the government secured 'almost complete control over the conditions of railway operation and hours of labour' [Alderman, 1973: *177*], and railway managers were left with rising labour costs at a time of frozen rates and general inflation.

In this situation it is scarcely surprising that labour relations were strained in the early twentieth century. Railway managements had always been paternalistic in attitude and contemptuous of union activity. Their reluctance to alter wage-rates and backsliding on working hours — the effectiveness of the 1893 Act was weakened considerably as business picked up after 1900 [Bagwell, 1963: *171–2*] — provoked inevitable reactions from organised labour as the cost of living began to rise. The Taff Vale Railway strike of 1900, which was followed by a successful claim for damages by the employers, was only one of several local disputes. Union membership grew rapidly: that of the Amalgamated Society of Railway Servants (ASRS), the largest union, increased from 38,000 in 1895 to 98,000 in 1907, the year in which demands for higher rates, shorter hours and, above all, recognition, reached a crescendo. Lloyd George, President of the Board of Trade, intervened to avert a strike, but the resulting conciliation and arbitration scheme appeared to favour the railway companies. Recognition was not conceded, and average wages in 1910 were a penny *less* than in 1907, at a time of rising prices and rising railway profits. A national strike in August 1911 stimulated fresh initiatives. The unions secured a modest increase in wage-rates – average wages were 6 per cent higher in 1912 than in 1910 – and an improvement in the system of collective bargaining. In return, the restraint on railway charges imposed by the 1894 Act was relaxed to permit limited increases to offset additional labour costs (Railway and Canal Traffic Act, 1913).

The story of labour relations to 1914 thus appears to be one of a successful resistance by hard-pressed employers. By no means all wage-rates were raised – those of engine-drivers on the South Eastern, for example, were not changed from 1890 to 1919 [Gourvish, 1979(a): 28] – and a 60-hour week remained the industry's norm. Furthermore, *full* union recognition was still denied, while sectionalism was encouraged by the abolition in 1911 of the Central Conciliation Boards [Bagwell, 1963: 303]. However, it is also clear that the companies made significant concessions in collective bargaining, both in 1907 and 1911 [Alderman, 1973: 199, 212]. And Lloyd George's promised *quid pro quo* in 1907 – a more sympathetic treatment of railway combination – did not materialise when three of the largest companies, the Great Northern, Great Eastern, and Great Central, presented a bill for a complete working union in 1909 [Cain, 1972: 631–7].

The companies were able to make some progress in the years after 1900. They secured a greater measure of inter-company co-operation and a more effective use of labour and equipment in their freight operations. But in general the period was a bleak one. Government intervention, once piecemeal and lukewarm, had penetrated all areas of managerial activity. It had resulted in restrictions on pricing and a rise in labour costs. Above all, it had helped to transform industrial relations. The strength of the National Union of Railwaymen, the successor of the ASRS and 273,000-strong in 1914, was in part, at least, a reflection of the attitude of successive governments and the Board of Trade to working conditions.

Does the extension of government control after 1870 suggest that the influence of the much-publicised 'Railway Interest' was exaggerated? Certainly the 'Interest', here defined (after Bagwell [1965] and Alderman [1973]) as the group of railway directors in Parliament, excited a great deal of contemporary criticism of its alleged political power. And its numerical strength built up impressively from the 1840s. In 1841 there were only 13 railway-director MPs, but by 1847 there were 80, and by 1866 the figure had risen to a peak of 215 (including 53 in the House of Lords). However, numbers by themselves are misleading. Alderman rightly distinguishes between total representation and the 'efficient interest', a much smaller group of about 60 MPs who were directors of the large, national railway companies. Moreover, the active leadership of the interest was more narrowly confined to a handful of committed lobbyists, men such as Sir Daniel Gooch (Great Western) and Sir Edward Watkin (South Eastern) whose business careers were closely if not totally bound up in the industry.

How successful, then, was this more narrowly-based group in defending the railways from government interference? It does seem that the 'interest' was at its most effective before it really existed in an organisational sense. Unity and purpose were scarcely characteristics of the railways' parliamentary activities until the formation of the United Railway Companies' Committee in 1867 (from 1870 the Railway Companies' Association), and this body was not fully representative until the mid-1870s. Nevertheless, it was in the 1840s and 1850s that a more loosely-organised group, brought together on an *ad hoc* basis and led by influential men such as George Hudson and George Carr Glyn, was able to restrict the ambitions of government legislation. Notable successes included the important amendments to Gladstone's bill of 1844, and the limitation of the scope of the Railway and Canal Traffic Act of 1854 [Alderman, 1973: *16–18*]. Here the growing numerical strength of the railway interest was not the crucial factor. Railways were advantaged by the lack of a clear railway policy within governmental circles and the absence of a strong party loyalty in both Liberal and Tory ranks. It only needed a few determined voices raised in protest to influence the course of railway legislation, particularly if the appeal was made on behalf of the 'freedom of commercial enterprise'.

However, the climate of opinion changed rapidly in the 1870s, as we have seen. Nowhere was this more apparent than in the magazine *Punch*. While in 1846 it could refer to the railways in rather jocular fashion as a 'Fifth Estate', it was by 1873 advising its readers that the industry was far too strong in the House of Commons, and that they should on no account vote for 'a Railway Chairman, Director, [or] Official of any kind'. In the eighties and nineties its pages were full of cartoons depicting overcrowded trains and overworked signalmen.[16] Thus while the size of the railway interest in Parliament was not greatly diminished — as late as 1900 there were 134 MPs, 71 of them representing the major companies — its position was progressively weakened as successive governments, faced with the strident criticisms of traders, farmers and industrialists, were forced to grasp the nettle of control.

This is not to say that the 'Railway Interest' had no success after 1870. With its collective voice increasingly represented by the Railway Companies' Association, it secured amendments to the Railway and Canal Traffic Act of 1873, put on a brave face before the Select Committee on Rates of 1881, and resisted compulsion in safety legislation until ready to yield. But intransigence was in the long run counter-productive. Increasing impatience with the railways undoubtedly influenced the harsher climate of the late eighties, and the industry won no friends for its attitude to freight rates in the early 1890s. As the Liberal Party became more closely identified with the interests of trade, railway directors were driven into the ranks of the Conservatives. In 1868 no less than 63 per cent of the 'efficient interest' were Liberals or Liberal-sympathisers, but by 1914 the proportion had dwindled to 18 per cent [Alderman, 1973: *232–50*]. In the end, however, there was little comfort to be derived from the 'natural party of big business'. The special concerns of the railways were soon effectively submerged in those of industry and commerce as a whole. Liberal governments may have shown the sharper teeth, with the Railway Commission (1873), cheap trains (1883), working hours (1893), and rates (1894), but the Conservatives, while more anxious to consult with the companies, were certainly not opposed to legislative controls. Indeed it was they who introduced the Railway and Canal Traffic Act of 1888 and the safety measures of 1889 and 1900. The 'Railway Interest' might demonstrate and filibuster, but it could not stem the collectivist tide. By 1914, perhaps by 1900, its importance as an instrument of political resistance was at an end.

8 Conclusion

NOW that 150 years have passed since the Liverpool and Manchester Railway first opened its doors to the public, it is all too easy to underestimate the role of the railways in the Victorian economy. Railways were more than a technologically superior mode of transport which reduced costs and facilitated the speedier, more reliable movement of passengers and freight. They were also a major industry in their own right and the first example of large-scale enterprise in the United Kingdom. Their promotion and construction in the forty years after 1830 had important linkage effects on several industries — notably iron and coal — and helped to transform financial institutions and the habits of savers. Any dissatisfaction we may have with the 'social saving' method of calculating their impact should not lead us to minimise their undoubted contribution to economic growth in the mid-nineteenth century. And whatever their difficulties in the years after 1870, there can be no dispute about their continuing relevance to industrial and commercial development. It is true that in the period 1870–1914 we may find the origins of many of the industry's more enduring problems and, in particular, the obvious conflict between a 'market' approach to transport provision and the 'public service' environment encouraged by government and interest-groups. However, before 1914 these were largely masked by the companies' ability to provide reasonable returns for investors while at the same time they so clearly dominated inland transport.

Tabular Appendix

Table 1
A revised (low) estimate of social saving from the railways of England and Wales in 1865

1 Passenger traffic:

rail cost	non-rail cost (2.48d. per passenger-mile)	saving	saving as % of net national product England and Wales (£644m.)
£18.4m.	£23.0m.	£4.6m.	

2 Freight traffic:

rail cost	non-rail cost (1.75d. per ton-mile)		
£15.7m.	£22.8m.	£7.1m.	

3 Freight—additional savings:
Livestock and meat traffic £0.4m.
Supplementary wagon haulage £5.0m.

Total:		£17.1m.	2.66

Assumptions:
1. Passenger rail cost is £12.5m. plus costs of an additional 557 million passenger-miles of road transport to and from rail stations (c. 3 miles on top of an average journey of c. 12 miles), distributed *pro rata* among first-class (4d. per mile), second (2½d.), and third (2d.).
2. Passenger non-rail cost based on comparison of first-class with 'inside' coach at 4d. per mile, second with 'outside' coach at 2½d., and third (including seasons) with 'outside' coach at 2d. (adjusted for journeys by canal and sea).

3. Freight non-rail cost based on canal costs at 0.4*d.* per ton-mile plus shipping costs at 1.35*d.*
4. Livestock and meat traffic: Hawke's lower estimate is used.
5. Supplementary wagon haulage: assumed that half of the savings were matched by wagon-haul to and from rail stations.
6. Net national product: 81% of Feinstein's (1972) figure of £795m. for the UK in 1865.

Table 2
A revised (high) estimate of social saving in 1865

1 Passenger traffic:

rail cost	non-rail cost (13.8*d.* per passenger-mile)	saving	saving as % of net national product England and Wales (£644m.)
£12.5m.	£128.2m.	£115.7m.	
Time-savings:		£1.0m.	

2 Freight traffic:

Savings as in ch. 5, Table III	£28.1m.	
Parcels, luggage, mails, etc.	£1.5m.	
Inventory savings (additional)	£1.0m.	
Total	£147.3m.	22.87

Assumptions:
1. Passenger non-rail cost based on comparison of first- and second-class rail including season tickets with posting (2*s.* per mile), third with 'inside'/'outside' coach at 3.25*d.* per mile.
2. Time-savings: 30 mph rail 10 mph coach, for 445.69 million passenger-miles, at £2 per 60 hours saved.
3. Parcels, etc.: assumes non-rail costs are double rail costs.
4. Inventory savings: double Hawke's estimate.

Notes and References

1. Charles Dickens, 'A Flight', in *Reprinted Pieces* (Chapman and Hall: 1868 edn) p. 238.
2. A. D. Chandler, Jnr, 'The Railroads: Pioneers in Modern Corporate Management', *Business History Review*, XXXI (1965).
3. Deane's estimates of fixed capital formation suggest a railway share of 55 per cent, 1845–9, but Feinstein [1978, *32–4*] claims that these seriously underestimate the level of capital formation before the mid-1850s. His own estimate for 1841–50, while equally conjectural, is 46 per cent higher than Deane's for the same period.
4. *Railway Returns*, P.P. 1871, LX.
5. South Eastern Railway Board Minutes, 25 June 1868, RAIL 635/39, Public Record Office.
6. Employment estimates were derived from a regression of employment on UK lines under construction on expenditure on way and works (Mitchell's figures, incorporating his recommended adjustments for 1845–51) for 1847–60:

$$\text{Log}\overline{\text{E}} = 8.36178 + 1.18214 \log W, \text{ where } W = \text{expenditure}$$
$$(47.8672) \qquad (15.1915)$$

on way and works. Figures in parenthesis = T ratios. $r^2 = 0.950$.

7. Alternative calculations are available in Riden [1980, *82–3*]. These combine Hawke's data with Vamplew's (but including the latter's estimates of the demand for iron for rolling-stock), and compare the results with Riden's estimates of pig-iron output and home sales.
8. Pig-iron consumption was taken to be 3,466,000 tons (Mitchell's estimate plus 25 per cent), and *total* coal needs for the conversion from ore to wrought-iron and so on at 7 tons for each ton of pig-iron. UK coal production was taken to be between 250 and 380 million tons, 1844–51. I am indebted to Roy Church for his help with this calculation.
9. For 1844–51 UK engine-mileage was estimated at 429 million (300 million train-miles × 143/100), with fuel consumption at 40 lb coke (57 lb coal) per engine-mile. For UK coal output see note 8. For 1862–6 engine-mileage was taken to be 909.5 million (636m. × 143/100), with coal consumption at 50 lb per engine-mile. UK coal output was 460.5 million tons [Mitchell and Deane 1962, *115*]. Constructional demand was estimated at c.2–2.5 million tons of pig-iron × 7 (cf. note 8).
10. Percentages of 2.6 (1850) and 6.4 (1855) were derived from Hawke [1970, *48–50, 88–9*] (the freight savings were doubled to take account of additional savings). In these calculations we accept Hawke's contention that for 1850–64 a linear transition from Lardner's comparisons (passenger estimate 1) to those of the Royal Commission of 1867 (estimate 2) should be assumed. However, if the latter estimate were used throughout, the social saving would be raised to 6.7 per cent in 1850 and 8.5 per cent in 1855.

11. The calculation is based on preliminary freight savings of £65.5m. [Hawke: 1970, 89] doubled for additional savings; savings of £191m. on 6,500 million passenger-miles [ibid., 301], with non-rail cost taken to be 8.13d. at constant prices; and net national income as £1,122m. (81 per cent of £1,385m.).
12. N. M. Mason, 'Unprofitable Railway Companies in England and Wales, 1870–1914', paper read to the Transport History Group Conference, Bristol Polytechnic, September 1979.
13. Quoted in J. Tatlow, *Fifty Years of Railway Life* (1920) p. 104.
14. Samuel Laing, letter to Sir Edward Watkin, 1 July 1885, in South Eastern Board Minutes, 16 July 1885, RAIL 635/49, Public Record Office.
15. Compliance was not quite as impressive as these figures suggest. In 1889 (30 June) the proportion of locomotives and carriages actually fitted with *brakes* (as opposed to brake apparatus, pipes and so on) was 74 per cent, with 60 per cent using automatic types.
16. *Punch*, XI (1846) *111*; 15 November 1873, cited in Simmons [1978, *245*]; 6 October 1883; 28 January and 14 October 1893.

Select Bibliography

Place of publication is London unless otherwise stated. The abbreviation *EcHR* represents the *Economic History Review*, second series, and *JTH* The *Journal of Transport History*.

Aldcroft, D. H., 'The Efficiency and Enterprise of British Railways, 1870–1914', *Explorations in Entrepreneurial History*, v (1968(a)).
——, *British Railways in Transition* (1968(b)).
——, 'Railways and Economic Growth', *JTH*, n.s.I (1972).
Alderman, G., 'The Railway Companies and the Growth of Trade Unionism in the late Nineteenth and early Twentieth Centuries', *Historical Journal*, XIV (1971(a)).
——, 'The Victorian Transport Revolution', *Historical Journal*, XIV (1971(b)).
——, *The Railway Interest* (Leicester, 1973).
Ashworth, W., *An Economic History of England, 1870–1939* (1960).
Atkins, P. J., 'The Growth of London's Milk Trade, c. 1845–1914', *JTH*, n.s.IV (1978).
Bagwell, P. S., *The Railwaymen* (1963).
——, 'The Railway Interest: its Organisation and Influence 1839–1914', *JTH*, VII (1965).
——, *The Railway Clearing House in the British Economy 1842–1922* (1968).
——, *The Transport Revolution From 1770* (1974).
Barker, T. C. and Robbins, M., *A History of London Transport* (2 vols, 1963, 1974).
Barker, T. C. and Savage, C. I., *An Economic History of Transport in Britain* (1974).
Baxter, R. D., 'Railway Expansion and its Results', *Journal of the Statistical Society*, XXIX (1866), reprinted in E. M. Carus-Wilson (ed.), *Essays in Economic History*, vol. III (1962).
Broadbridge, S., *Studies in Railway Expansion and the Capital Market in England 1825–1873* (1970).
Cain, P. J., 'Railway Combination and Government, 1900–1914', *EcHR*, XXV (1972).

Cain, P. J., 'Traders versus Railways: The Genesis of the Railway and Canal Traffic Act of 1894', *JTH*, n.s.II (1973).
——, 'The British Railway Rates Problem 1894–1913', *Business History*, XX (1978).
Chaloner, W. H., *The Social and Economic Development of Crewe, 1780–1923* (Manchester, 1950).
Channon, G., 'The Aberdeenshire Beef Trade with London: a Study in Steamship and Railway Competition 1850–69', *Transport History*, II (1969).
——, 'A Nineteenth-Century Investment Decision: The Midland Railway's London Extension', *EcHR*, XXV (1972).
Church, R. A., 'The Railway Age: A Reinterpretation', *Midland History*, I (1971).
——, *The Great Victorian Boom 1850–1873* (Economic History Society, 1975).
Clapham, J. H., *An Economic History of Modern Britain*, vols I–II (Cambridge, 1926, 1932).
Cottrell, P. L., 'Railway Finance and the Crisis of 1866: Contractors' Bills of Exchange, and the Finance Companies', *JTH*, n.s.III (1976).
Deane, P., 'New Estimates of Gross National Product for the United Kingdom 1830–1914', *Review of Income and Wealth*, XIV (1968).
Dyos, H. J., *Victorian Suburb: A Study of the Growth of Camberwell* (Leicester, 1961).
Dyos, H. J. and Aldcroft, D. H., *British Transport* (Leicester, 1969).
Engerman, S. L., 'Railways and Economic Growth in England and Wales 1840–1870', *Business History*, XIII (1971).
Feinstein, C. H., *National Income, Expenditure and Output of the United Kingdom 1855–1965* (Cambridge, 1972).
——, 'Capital Formation in Great Britain', in P. Mathias and M. M. Postan (eds), *The Cambridge Economic History of Europe*, vol. VII, pt 1 (Cambridge, 1978).
Findlay, G., *The Working and Management of an English Railway* (1889).
Fishlow, A., *American Railroads and the Transformation of the Ante-Bellum Economy* (Cambridge, USA, 1965).
Floud, R., review of Hawke [1970], *History*, LVII (1972).
Fogel, R. W., *Railroads and American Economic Growth* (Baltimore, 1964).
Frankel, M., 'Obsolescence and Technological Change in a Mature

Economy', *American Economic Review*, XLV (1955).
Fremdling, R., 'Railroads and German Economic Growth', *Journal of Economic History*, XXXVII (1977).
Gourvish, T. R. and Reed, M. C., 'The Financing of Scottish Railways before 1860 – a Comment', *Scottish Journal of Political Economy*, XVIII (1971).
Gourvish, T. R., *Mark Huish and the London & North Western Railway* (Leicester, 1972).
———, 'A British Business Elite: The Chief Executive Managers of the Railway Industry, 1850–1922', *Business History Review*, XLVII (1973).
———, 'The Performance of British Railway Management After 1860: The Railways of Watkin and Forbes', *Business History*, XX (1978).
———, 'The Standard of Living, 1890–1914', in A. O'Day (ed.), *The Edwardian Age: Conflict and Stability 1900–1914* (1979(a)).
———, 'Les dirigeants salariés de l'industrie des chemins de fer britanniques, 1850–1922', in M. Levy–Leboyer (ed.), *Le Patronat de la seconde industrialisation* (Paris, 1979(b)).
———, 'Railway Enterprise', in R. A. Church (ed.), *The Dynamics of Victorian Business* (1980).
Hawke, G. R., 'Pricing Policy of Railways in England and Wales Before 1881', in Reed [1969].
Hawke, G. R. and Reed, M. C., 'Railway Capital in the United Kingdom in the Nineteenth Century', *EcHR*, XXII (1969).
Hawke, G. R., *Railways and Economic Growth in England and Wales 1840–1870* (Oxford, 1970).
Hughes, J. R. T., *Fluctuations in Trade, Industry and Finance: A Study of British Economic Development 1850–1860* (Oxford, 1960).
Hyde, C. K., *Technological Change and the British Iron Industry 1700–1870* (Princeton, 1977).
Irving, R. J., 'British Railway Investment and Innovation 1900–1914', *Business History*, XIII (1971).
———, *The North Eastern Railway Company 1870–1914* (Leicester, 1976).
———, 'The Profitability and Performance of British Railways, 1870–1914', *EcHR*, XXXI (1978).
Jackman, W. T., *The Development of Transportation in Modern England* (1916; new edn, 1962).
Jefferys, J. B., 'The Denomination and Character of Shares, 1855–

1885', *EcHR*, XVI (1946), reprinted in E. M. Carus-Wilson (ed.), *Essays in Economic History*, vol. I (1954).
Jenks, L. H., 'Railroads as an Economic Force in American Development', *Journal of Economic History*, IV (1944), reprinted in E. M. Carus-Wilson, (ed.), *Essays in Economic History*, vol. III (1962).
Kellett, J. R., *The Impact of Railways on Victorian Cities* (1969).
Kenwood, A. G., 'Railway Investment in Britain, 1825–1875', *Economica*, n.s. XXXII (1965).
Kindleberger, C. P., 'Obsolescence and Technical Change', *Bulletin of the Oxford University Institute of Statistics*, XXIII (1961).
Lardner, D., *Railway Economy* (1850).
Lee, C. H., *The Quantitative Approach to Economic History* (1977).
McCloskey, D. N., review of Hawke [1970], *EcHR*, XXIV (1971).
Matthews, R. C. O., *A Study in Trade Cycle History: Economic Fluctuations in Great Britain 1833–1842* (Cambridge, 1954).
Mitchell, B. R. and Deane, P., *Abstract of British Historical Statistics* (Cambridge, 1962).
Mitchell, B. R., 'The Coming of the Railway and United Kingdom Economic Growth', *Journal of Economic History*, XXIV (1964), reprinted in Reed [1969].
O'Brien, P., *The New Economic History of the Railways* (1977).
Paish, G., *The British Railway Position* (1902).
Parris, H., *Government and the Railways in Nineteenth-Century Britain* (1965).
Perkin, H., *The Age of the Railway* (1970).
Perren, R., 'The Meat and Livestock Trade in Britain, 1850–70', *EcHR*, XXVIII (1975).
Pollard, S. and Marshall, J. D., 'The Furness Railway and the Growth of Barrow', *JTH*, I (1953).
Pollins, H., 'The Marketing of Railway Shares in the First Half of the Nineteenth Century', *EcHR*, VII (1954).
———, 'Railway Contractors and the Finance of Railway Development in Britain', *JTH*, III (1957–8), reprinted in Reed [1969].
———, *Britain's Railways* (Newton Abbot, 1971).
Reader, W. J., *Professional Men* (1966).
Reed, M. C., (ed.), *Railways in the Victorian Economy* (Newton Abbot, 1969).
———, *Investment in Railways in Britain 1820–1844* (Oxford, 1975).

Riden, P. J., 'The Iron Industry', in R. A. Church (ed.), *The Dynamics of Victorian Business* (1980).
Rostow, W. W., *The Process of Economic Growth* (Oxford, 1960).
Saul, S. B., review of Hawke [1970], *Business History Review*, XLV (1971).
Saville, J., 'Sleeping Partnerships and Limited Liability, 1850–1856', *EcHR*, VIII (1956).
Shannon, H. A., 'The Coming of General Limited Liability', *Economic History*, II (1931), reprinted in E. M. Carus-Wilson (ed.), *Essays in Economic History*, vol. I (1954).
Simmons, J., *The Railway in England and Wales 1830–1914*, vol. I (Leicester, 1978).
Thompson, F. M. L., *Chartered Surveyors: The Growth of a Profession* (1968).
Turnbull, G. L., *Traffic and Transport: An Economic History of Pickfords* (1979).
Vamplew, W., 'The Railways and the Iron Industry: A Study of Their Relationship in Scotland', in Reed [1969].
——, 'Nihilistic Impressions of British Railway History', in D. N. McCloskey (ed.), *Essays on a Mature Economy: Britain after 1840* (1971).
Wilson, H. Raynar, *Railway Accidents, Legislation and Statistics 1825 to 1924* (1925).

Index

Aberdeen 30
accidents 50—3
  Armagh (1889) 52
accounting 10, 51
Acts of Parliament, private 29, 49—50
Acts of Parliament, public
  Cheap Trains (1883) 48, 52, 56
  Railway & Canal Traffic (1854) 50, 55
  Railway & Canal Traffic (1873) 48, 51, 56
  Railway & Canal Traffic (1888) 47—8, 51, 56
  Railway & Canal Traffic (1894) 46—8, 54, 56
  Railway & Canal Traffic (1913) 54
  Railway Clauses Consolidation (1845) 50
  Railway Regulation (1893) 46, 53, 56
  Regulation of Railways (1844) 15, 50, 55
  Regulation of Railways (1868) 43, 51
  Regulation of Railways (1889) 52, 56
agents, parliamentary 22
Aldcroft, Derek 43—7
amalgamations 27, 49—52, 54
Associated Society of Railway Servants 53—4

banks 18—19
Barrow 31
Baxter, Dudley 39
Board of Trade 49, 51—4
Brassey, Thomas 21
Brunel, Isambard 21
brick industry 25

canals 26—30, 34—9, 49, 58—9
  Kennet & Avon 38
  Leeds & Liverpool 38
capital expenditure 16, 18—20, 27—8, 41, 44—6, 60
capital market 14—19, 33, 39
carriers 26, 30
Cazenove, Henry 18
Clapham, John 17, 27, 33
coaches, road 26, 29, 58—9
coal industry 25, 31—3, 41, 45, 57, 60
  traffic 26—8, 30, 35
coastal shipping 26—8, 30, 34
communication cord 51—2
concentration, company 10, 27, 49—51, 54
conciliation and arbitration 53—4
Conservative Party 55—6
construction 20—5, 49, 57
contractors 16, 18
costs 45—6, 53
costing 10, 29, 44
Crewe 25, 31
cross-subsidisation 44

67

Dalhousie, Lord 50
debentures 18
Dickens, Charles 9

economic growth 13−15, 33−40, 57
'economic performance' 41−8, 54
Edinburgh 17
engineering 21, 25, 33
exports 24−5, 33

Forbes, James Staats 45, 47
Foster & Braithwaite 18
freight traffic 9, 26−31, 34−7, 41, 44−7, 54, 56, 58−9

Gladstone, William 15, 50, 55
Glasgow 17
Glyn, George Carr 19, 55
Gooch, Sir Daniel 55
Gorton 31
government control 11, 27−8, 44, 46−57
Gray, Thomas 49
Grisewood, Harman 19

Hawke, Gary 12−13, 16, 23−4, 28−30, 33−41, 59
Heseltine Powell 18
holiday resorts 31
Hudson, George 17, 55
Huish, Mark 28

industrial location 31, 35
insurance companies 18
inventories 26, 35, 37, 59
investment 9−10, 12−19, 33, 35, 41−2, 44−5

iron industry 20, 22−5, 31, 33, 35, 40, 57, 60
South Wales 24, 31

labour 9−10, 20−2, 31, 35, 39, 60
conditions 53−4
costs 46−7, 53−4
relations 53−4
Lardner, Dionysius 30, 34, 37, 38
Laing, Samuel 52
Leeds 17
Liberal Party 55−6
limited liability 10, 17−18, 49
Liverpool 17
livestock traffic 30, 34, 37, 58
Lloyd George, David 53−4
Locke, Joseph 21
London 9, 27−8, 30, 45
luggage traffic 34, 59

management 10, 27−9, 35, 39, 41, 44, 46−7, 53−4
Manchester 17
'mania' 9−10, 12−16, 22, 28, 50
Middlesborough 31
mileage, railway 9, 16, 20, 41−2
mineral traffic 30, 35
Mitchell, Brian 12−13, 17, 20, 22−5, 27−8, 33, 39
Morrison, John 49
multiplier effects 21

national income 13, 21, 34−7, 39, 41, 58−9
National Union of Railwaymen 54

68

Neilson's hot-blast   23

operating margins   27–8, 30, 44, 46, 52
'operating ratio'   42–3, 45–6
operation   26–32, 44–8
organisation   10–11
Overend, Gurney 'crash'   19, 21

parcels traffic   34, 59
Paris   9
passenger, traffic   9, 26–7, 29–30, 34–7, 41, 44, 47, 50–2, 58–9
perishable goods traffic   30–1, 41
postal services   31, 34, 59
posting   34, 59
pressure groups   44, 47–8, 51, 56–7
pricing   26–7, 29–30, 35, 44, 46, 49, 54
productivity   28–9, 43, 54
professions   21–2
profits   15–16, 27–8, 42, 45–6, 50, 52–3
Punch   55–6

quality of service   29, 32, 34, 38, 44–5, 47, 52

Railway and Canal Commission (1888–)   51
Railway Board (1844–5)   50
Railway Clearing House   27, 29
Railway Commission (1873–88)   51, 56
Railway Commissioners (1846–51)   50

railway companies
  Great Central   54
  Great Eastern   50, 54
  Great Northern   54
  Great Western   10, 50, 55
  Lancashire & Yorkshire   51
  Liverpool & Manchester   9, 14, 57
  London & North Western   10, 25, 49–51
  London Brighton & South Coast   52
  London Chatham & Dover   47, 52
  Manchester Sheffield & Lincs   45
  Midland   10, 25, 49
  North Eastern   10, 47, 50
  South Eastern   9, 19, 45, 47, 52, 54–5
  Stockton & Darlington   9
Railway Companies' Association   55–6
Railway Department   49–53
'Railway Interest'   54–6
railway revenue   9–10, 20, 26–7, 42
rate of return   16, 28, 42–3, 57
rates and fares   29–30, 34–5, 39, 46, 49–53, 56
Rawson, Henry   19
retailing   30
Royal Commission on Railways (1865–7)   34, 51

safety   45, 47, 50–3, 56, 61
select committees
  Communication by Railways (1839)   49

69

select committees — *continued*
   Railway and Canal Bills (1852—3) 50
   Amalgamation of Railway Companies (1872) 30, 51
   Railways (Rates and Fares) (1881—2) 51, 56
shares 16—19
Smith and Forrest v *London and North Western Railway, etc.* (1899) 46
social rate of return 16, 35
'social saving' 29, 33—9, 41, 57—61
solicitors 22
state purchase option 15, 50
statistics 23, 38, 43

steel 25
Stephenson, Robert 21
stock exchanges 16—17
stockbrokers 18—19
Stratford (London) 31
strike (1911) 53—4
surveying 21—2
Swindon, New 31

Taff Vale Strike (1900) 53
technology 14, 27
telegraph 31
terminal charges 50—1
tradd unions 53—4
transport costs 26, 29—30, 33

urbanisation 31

wages, railway 46, 53—4